RACHEL ASHWELL'S
PAINTED STORIES

RACHEL ASHWELL'S
PAINTED STORIES

VINTAGE, DECORATING, THOUGHTS, AND WHIMSY

Illustrations by Ben Peck-Whiston

CICO BOOKS
LONDON NEW YORK

BEN PECK-WHISTON

Ben lives with his husband David and two precious pugs, Rosebud and
Walter (not forgetting their dearly missed first-born fur baby, Rupert),
nestled between the Peak District and Sherwood Forest in the UK. Art
and the world of make believe has always played a huge part in his life,
from playing with his Nana's vintage tomato box doll house, to admiring
and now displaying his grandfather's portraits. Ben has created and
painted using many different media over the years, but his favorite is
using the gentle hues of watercolor. Currently he works on whimsical
watercolor commissions as well as recreating Rachel's flea market finds
in doll house miniatures which are sold and loved around the world.

Published in 2021 by CICO Books
An imprint of Ryland Peters & Small Ltd
20–21 Jockey's Fields   341 E 116th St
London WC1R 4BW   New York, NY 10029

www.rylandpeters.com

10 9 8 7 6 5 4 3 2 1

A CIP catalog record for this book is available from
the Library of Congress and the British Library.

ISBN: 978 1 80065 006 0

Printed in China

Art and design direction by Rachel Ashwell

Editor: Martha Gavin
Art director: Sally Powell
Head of production: Patricia Harrington
Publishing manager: Penny Craig
Publisher: Cindy Richards

CONTENTS

INTRODUCTION

This book is my personal notebook, an insight to how I see, feel, and love.

It is for anyone who has an appreciation for beauty. It's where I share my meandering thoughts that are evoked by what my eyes see and what my heart feels. Some of my words may be of a practical matter, so you can understand the details and aesthetics that resonate with me. And some of my notes are more philosophical thoughts of mine or quotes from others whose words bring deeper meaning than the beauty that appears on the surface.

On these pages is everything that I love. I often see things poetically and as a gateway to my heart. I see objects for their inherent beauty but I also like to create a narrative in my mind of the story that presents itself to me. Maybe you will connect to my stories in this book or maybe it will inspire you to see life through a new lens.

Hopefully you will become aware that beautiful things can be seen both inside and out, creating more meaningful value.

I chose to express my notebook by way of sketches and art as I feel the mindfulness of handwork is timeless and more easily translatable for you to layer in your own thoughts into your authentic life.

So, whether poetic portraits or paintings by my favorite artists, or sketches of fabrics, vintage, furniture, lighting, and more, I hope you enjoy it and that it creates a feast for your eyes, heart, and soul. And a journey for your mind to wander through.

chapter 1
SANCTUARY FOR OUR HEARTS

I have made many nests of homes over the years, from rented flats in cities, to shacks on the beach, and larger havens for friends and families. California was where I raised my children and where my world of Shabby Chic began. My home there in Los Angeles is quintessentially Shabby Chic. A little bit country and a little bit English with a southern flair. It houses my bits and bobs and life's gatherings of things and memories.

humble fancy

In recent years, I felt a yearning to return to my roots in England. My soul was drawn to the rhythm of the seasons, and I found myself gravitating to the culture for a new source of inspiration. It was time for me to reconnect with the country I had left as a young woman.

My agenda was to rent temporarily, for perhaps six months, a cottage in the English countryside until I found my dream home, a story-book country farmhouse.

Two years later, having been unable to find my new nest, I am still in my rented cottage.

Life has taken many twists and turns from when I first stepped over the threshold of what has become my safe haven.

Even though the decorator in me would have liked to have put down more permanent roots of my own home, there has been a great lesson in non-attachment without compromising, creating a sanctuary for my heart.

Expecting my stay to be brief, I set up my "stepping-stone" home with little else other than a couple of suitcases of clothes, my most treasured books, and some other personal bits and bobs. Only shipping from Los Angeles my beloved white slipcovered Portobello sofa, a vintage French white carved leaning mirror, my mama's red paisley armchair, a mid-century modern leather and chrome ottoman, and my white painted dining table with raw wood chairs, their white denim seat cushions and back slipcovers. The beauty of this new beginning is that I had no emotional or materialistic baggage. No junk drawers or clothes I hadn't worn in years.

I frequented the local flea markets so little by little I filled in some blanks of necessities, knowing my left-behind treasures would eventually move with me. But I had no stress waiting to find the right treasures. I lived happily with the empty blanks until I found what was right for me. It is second nature for me to only bring home pieces that my heart responds to. I never doubt when I come across something that I love as I know I can trust my instincts.

I am always guided to create homes with the common threads that I value: beauty, comfort, function, whimsy, serenity, warmth.

"The power of finding beauty in the humblest things makes home happy and life lovely."

Louisa May Alcott

MY BIG ROOM IN MY LITTLE COTTAGE

When renting a home, there are always some decorative compromises, perhaps paint choices and floor finishes. Kitchens and bathrooms can be the most challenging. But I have had some of the most nurturing baths in my funny little bathroom. While I fantasize about all the changes I would make given the opportunity, my candles, music, and flowers satisfy my senses and bring me peace and calm regardless of the setting.

During my time in my "stepping-stone" home I was faced with long periods of time of isolation during the pandemic. Like everyone, I found myself having to navigate through emotional and practical transformations. I found that my daily practices of prayer, journaling, and long walks became anchors of structure in my days that became weeks and months. I discovered profound gratitude in all of the beauty that surrounded me. Making my bed with my beautiful sheets, handwashing my vintage china, and putting my soulful linens out to dry on the washing line became my walking meditation. Appreciating every detail of these treasures. Validating, never underestimating the value that creating a beautiful home with meaningful treasures gives us as a sanctuary for our hearts.

PRETTY PORCELAIN
Matching cup, saucer, and dessert plate.

English porcelain, when held up to the light, has a wonderful translucent quality, it's so delicate and elegant to drink from.

ALWAYS FLOWERS
Flowers from local farmers, for all seasons. Flea market found pitcher.

STASH
My stash of Shabby Chic books. Older ones from days gone by, I use them to re-inspire myself. My vision expands and evolves but my values stay the same.

VISUAL MEMORY
My memory board.

No matter how brief or long I stay in a nest, I always
create a memory board. It is is my visual journal, it
cannot be contrived. It's a sacred space to gather and
record visual memories that become my personal
tapestries to reflect upon. And as my life unfolds, I layer
today's memories over yesterday's, or I let go of some to
make space for new ones, special to only me. And when
I catch a glimpse, they inspire me and touch my soul,
reacquainting my past memories with memories of today.

LOVE YOU SPOON
Added emotion for roses
in a milk bottle.

Linens drying
in the wind

WASHING LINE

Everything about a clothesline gives me joy. The simple ritual of mindfully and carefully hanging out clothes and linens that have served us well. Sometimes I gaze at my clothesline, pondering the thought that all that is drying has a fresh start, taking on the energy of nature by way of the breeze and sun, which nurtures the fabrics in our lives, gently and respectfully.

creating my "stepping-stone" sanctuary

My step-by-steps to satisfy all my senses.

1. A visual harmony.

2. Soft to the touch.

3. Fragrance (Baies Diptyque candles, lemongrass atomizer)

4. Always music:

Soft classical
Opera
Sade
Enya
Adele
Andrea Bocelli
Celine Dion
Crystal Gayle
Dido

5. Cup of tea with shortbread cookies (and a movie):

MOVIES
Out of Africa
The Notebook
Eat Pray Love
Miss Potter
The Holiday
Mamma Mia
Nanny McPhee
Bridget Jones's Diary
A Star is Born
The Sound of Music
Notting Hill

BEAUTY ON BEAUTY, QUILTS DRYING
A walking meditative moment, so much to absorb. Charming quilts, rustic fencing surrounding wide open spaces, and a baby lamb.

MY UNIFORM
These boots have walked the globe.

chapter 2
MY LOVE OF VINTAGE

Home is a beautiful word, one that can evoke feelings of a safe sanctuary, both emotionally and practically. When speaking about a house, it's where life is lived and memories are made. Whether we live alone, with family, or with friends passing through, it's our private space where we dream and little by little our lives unfold.

My mantra of beauty, comfort, and function helps me to gather and curate the elements which, when layered together, reflect my soul, personality, and creative expression.

There are many threads of equal value to create these tapestries that decorate our homes. A large beautifully carved armoire can take center stage, housing heirlooms of linen or everyday china, while a petite, vulnerable timeworn table, with a simple lone bud in a vase, can be a treasured unsung hero giving life to a forgotten space.

I have always been drawn to sifting through and discovering new treasures that were once discarded as I visualize a new lease of life that can be had. I am always searching for unique pieces to decorate homes, from mansions to cottages, centuries old to contemporary, and while certain palettes, shapes, sizes, and styles play a role, the common thread over my decision of choosing something is beauty, regardless of the setting. Beauty can always find a home.

Sky blue

Vanilla

PASTEL VANITY

You don't always get what you want, and this piece had already been sold when I came across her. But I still took a moment to study her beauty, scale, ornate and simple balance, along with her perfect palette.

VINTAGE FURNITURE

I love the days when I go looking for treasured pieces of furniture at flea markets. I consider the search like casting characters for a movie. Each piece has a unique personality and contributes to the story in their own way. Some have star qualities, while others co-star or are even extras, quietly in the background. But all play a role, bringing layers of beauty and comfort into a home.

The search can be a daunting task, curating piece by piece what was once someone else's unwanted junk, finding that diamond in the rough. It takes patience and consideration but is so worthwhile when I stand back and gaze at the culmination of my gathers. My palette is cohesive, like the threads of a tapestry. A feminine frilly lampshade is as much of the story as a primitive bookcase, an intricately designed armoire, or a modest stool.

Lyrics from Pink's song "Just Give Me a Reason," are about a relationship not being broken, but just a little bit bent. The same applies to vintage furniture with their inevitable bends, cracks, and wonkiness. They just need to be found, restored, curated, and ready for a new love.

Over the years thousands of pieces of vintage furniture have passed through my gaze and, if chosen, into my hands, at least temporarily until each piece goes through my process of "restoring, ready for reloving" and on to others, unless it becomes a "forever-to-keep" for me.

My beacon of light as I search is my palette of celadon greens, seafoam to smoky teal, dusty rose, baby pink, and ravishing raspberry, faded gray to sky blue along with fifty shades of white, and then subtle hues of raw wood. I am as much captivated by a wonky distressed pink stool that may well have supported hours of meaningful conversation as an intricately carved Marie Antoinette vanity that has likely reflected prepping for a fancy ball.

On these next pages I will share with you some of my favorite pieces and my thoughts on why I love them. Maybe the colors might speak to you, or the little details that may often go unnoticed. To me, each one has their own gorgeousness, however bold or humble.

"Have nothing in your home that you do not know to be useful or believe to be beautiful."

William Morris

hodgepodge beauties

I've always considered the effort of searching for vintage treasures brings value to the overall appreciation when finally placed in its new home. The journeys of retrieving and stories passed down give objects personalities unto themselves and an inner beauty. And knowing they are usually one-of-a-kind finds makes them all the more special versus the anonymity of mass-produced furniture.

THE TRIO
All serving a very different function but each equally as important as the others.

SMOKY GREEN GLASS FRONT HUTCH

Scallop header

DENIM BLUE PAINTED ARMOIRE

TALL SIX-DRAWER DRESSER

Beadboard back

Wood drawer handles

BLUSH CABINET

Wallpaper shelves

Kate Winslet's character in **The Holiday** talks about healing from a broken heart, feeling insignificant and not seen, but over time little pieces of her soul come back. I see rescuing a discarded piece of vintage in the same way, nurturing it and bringing it back, and its soul returns to once again be a piece of value in new and appreciative hands.

1940S PASTEL HUTCH

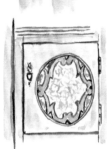

Blue interior

Plank back

Debossed glass

Bun feet

DRESSY DRAWER
Sometimes the floral décor is added later in life, but when done well—not too precious and a little smudgy—it's a welcomed decorative addition.

HUNGARIAN PRINCESS
I've bought many vintage cabinets originating from Hungary. Typically quite primitive and chunky, often with crudely painted flowers.

Raw unpainted top

Lavender flowers

Chunky molding and carvings

Bun feet

Gray squiggles

Light handed floral decoration

Cup handles

tips and tricks

Part of my "restoring, ready for reloving" process is making sure a vintage treasure is functional and honoring its timeworn and faded character. I am careful when choosing elements to refresh that I do so sympathetically with the history and aesthetic inherent within the piece. Once a piece is restored, it should feel like its soul has been restored.

MODESTY & GRACE
Faded hues of blue with a marble top and caster wheels which contribute to her specialness.

I'm drawn to the many shades of blue, perhaps because it spiritually symbolizes peace, truth, and tranquility.

MAGICAL MARBLE
A slab of mellow marble always adds value, and is well appreciated when found on a vintage treasure. Often the edges are rounded and double beveled. At times when I make the decision to add a marble surface, specifically for a bathroom or kitchen piece, I always choose a honed (non-shiny finish) with soft or clean edges for a more modern aesthetic. (Bevel is usually too expensive a detail today.)

DETAILS
The details of hardware are of utmost importance. Sometimes a dresser only calls for a simple wonky knob, or a tarnished lacy metal handle. Sometimes just a simple worn bronze pull will do. But whatever it is, the piece directs what would complement it best. Caster wheels are always a welcome addition. At times I add them if extra height is needed. I'm always grateful when the hardware comes intact, even if it's sometimes mismatched from a prior loss. But if missing or wrongly placed along the way, I always take the time to source vintage hardware to restore it to what it feels like it would have been, once upon a time.

Porcelain and crystal knobs

Simple but graceful lines of metal handle

Pressed metal leaf design within dainty form

Caster wheels

Mellowed-with-age drawer pull

PAINT & PALETTE

It's always my preference to keep discovered treasures as I find them in their authentic patina and palette, but if for some reason paint touch up or smudges are needed, I work within a specific range of colors. Many shades of white (avoiding creamy white), taupe, blues, teal, and of course pink.

Blush

Dove   Tea stain

Fawn   Malibu blue

Clay   Mist

Mink   Truly teal

SHABBY CHIC

SHABBY CHIC

LINING DRAWERS

Lining drawers, shelves, and cabinets with vintage wallpaper takes little effort and brings such joy to the ordinary idea of decorating where we keep our everyday things.

farmhouse

I love vintage farmhouse furniture. I've always pondered on the hands that made them and their acceptance of the inevitable imperfections. The hidden details made with humility, like dowels and screws which are often never seen, are the strength and support. Layers of paint, often diverse, as each piece passes through the chapters of life.

TABLE FOR ALL REASONS

Around the table, the most valuable conversations are often had. The comfort of food or a cup of tea can create an easy atmosphere leading to intimate and meaningful conversation.

The duck egg blue, authentically weathered table was a tad short, so I popped on a set of caster wheels. In time I added a marble slab over the top as it serves as a kitchen island in my home, so along with a mix of three stools, it makes for easy moving around as needed.

Embroidered pillow

Caster wheels

SOULFULLY AGED STOOL

Sometimes things cross our paths that we love more than they might warrant. But there is just something special about them. I believe sometimes we pick up on the legacy of the life already lived. This pink crackled stool with her tall and slender frame feels graceful but also embodies a secure strength.

THE ORDINARY CHAIR

I have had this pale turquoise chair for years and years. She has been shuffled from house to house, office to office. Sometimes grouped with others, sometimes she's the one and only, tucked away, bringing purpose to a corner. My "forever-to-keep."

Mushy floral linen chair pad with rumpled ties

Sometimes it's things that are not extraordinary that are so special. They are inviting and unintimidating, because they are just what they are, in confidence without judgment of self or others.

Decorative carved back

Spindle back

Rounded seat

Primitive, simple form with thin floppy cushion

Round edged rectangle seat

MUSICAL CHAIRS

I love a variety of mix-and-match wooden chairs, paired with a selection of comfy cushions. If only they could talk and share their history.

Always check for sturdiness of legs and back spindles (often a dab of glue will make good).

HANDSOME WITH A FEMININE TOUCH

Bows

PRETTY & PRIMITIVE
Likely the maker of this bench never
expected it to be graced with a
beautiful, squishy cushion elevating
her to her next chapter in life.

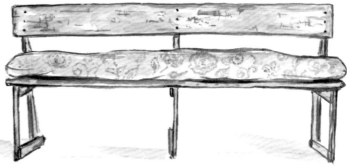

BASIC & BEAUTIFUL
I've often bought benches with an idea of purpose,
perhaps for extra seating, but over time they move
around, perhaps as a coffee table, or console behind
a settee, or a plopping place in a hallway. They are
not defined by the space where they land up, but
simply by their value.

SEAT FOR THREE
No need for cushions. But if
I changed my mind, I would
add a long bench seat.

Original hardware

Raw wood top

Chunky countertop

Drawer pulls

Multiple deep drawers

Beadboard cabinet fronts

HEAVY & HANDSOME

Just as Brandi Carlile sings about the lines of imperfections on her face which tell her story, the nicks, bruises, and scuffs on a vintage piece are evidence of the story of their life.

This heavy and handsome sideboard I found in Texas is full of soul. Completely practical as well as being such a significant presence. In a kitchen I always try to piece together free-standing vintage pieces. Often, they are handmade with detail and qualities of days gone by. I like the personality they bring rather than the uniformity of all built-in units.

Sometimes pieces come with the hardware missing, in which case I look to find original replacements, but sometimes the hardware just needs to be cleaned up and oiled.

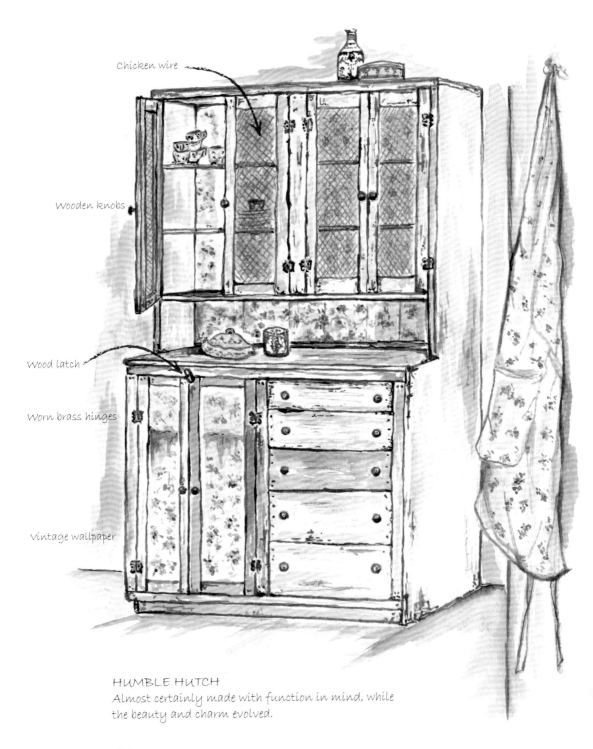

Chicken wire

Wooden knobs

Wood latch

Worn brass hinges

Vintage wallpaper

HUMBLE HUTCH
Almost certainly made with function in mind, while
the beauty and charm evolved.

TRULY TURQUOISE

The most basic lines and details, with handsome proportions. Clearly made with love by hand many years ago. Layers of paint add character with ease.

Tiny precious wood latch

grand and gorgeous

By the nature of their size, armoires, hutches, and large cabinets are often the anchor of a room. They bring a presence to their setting. Their patina may blend into other furnishings or they may contribute a layer of texture and soul into a more modern or minimal setting. I love the individuality they bring into a room. The ones I buy were often handmade before built-in cabinetry was commonplace in homes. Because they were likely handmade, they have a sensible functionality to them. Sometimes I make tweaks to their function, I may replace a pole in lieu of shelves in an armoire.

The "restoring, ready for reloving" process takes some time. Often these pieces can be a little grungy, especially if their prior life was in a kitchen. So, to start they may just need a good clean. But, be careful not to clean off the patina or original paint. If paint is a little flakey, go over with a non-yellowing, matt sealer. I like to line shelves or cabinets with vintage wallpaper, just to add some specialness.

If all the hardware has to be replaced, I try to find complete sets of authentic vintage hardware. But if only a couple pieces need replacing, I usually only replace those as I don't mind mixing hardware.

Drawers and cabinet fronts may have to be realigned if their life's journey has made them wonky. Occasionally I may have a handyman replace backs or bottoms of drawers with new plywood. (Always keep an eye out for a mass of tiny holes. These could be termites and can be often irreparable and also spreadable in your home if not treated.)

Don't feel restricted by placing a fancy French armoire in a bedroom or a primitive pantry cupboard in the kitchen. I love to place things in unexpected situations. I have a Marie Antoinette armoire, probably in a boudoir in a past life, now housing table linens in a dining room. And a simple beauty cabinet with evidence of prior kitchen use is now the keeper of bathroom towels and linens on an upstairs landing.

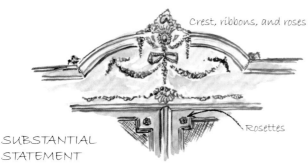

Crest, ribbons, and roses

Rosettes

SUBSTANTIAL STATEMENT

Formal carving and scale contribute to his commanding presence. But not intimidating due to his worn patina and tarnished hardware.

Taupe trim

BELLE OF THE BALL
Who is the fairest, impossible to choose?
Either French or Italian. Truly magnificent.

Duck egg blue

Poles, although could
be replaced with shelves
if preferred

Pastel hand-
painted flowers

Delicate carved legs

Sweeping header with scallop carving

Light sage green

Elegant handles
decorated with
curtain tassel

timeworn embellishments

Rubbed-down rose carvings and faded painted flowers
are treasures to be treasured. Fanciful embellishments
fading gracefully.

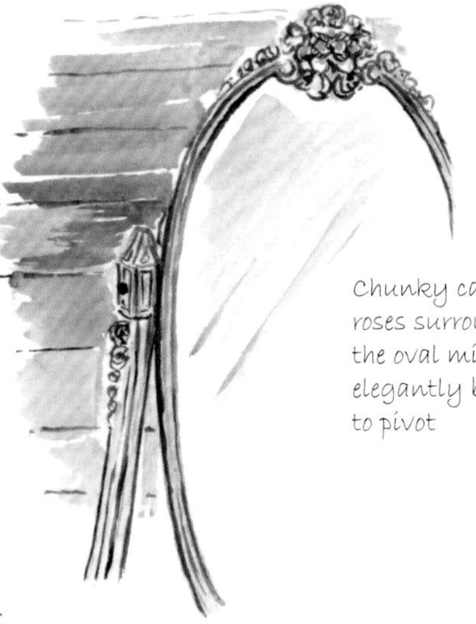

FEAST FOR THE EYES
On first glance, this was a "forever-to-keep"
for me. There is so much to her although she
speaks softly with her tattered elegance.

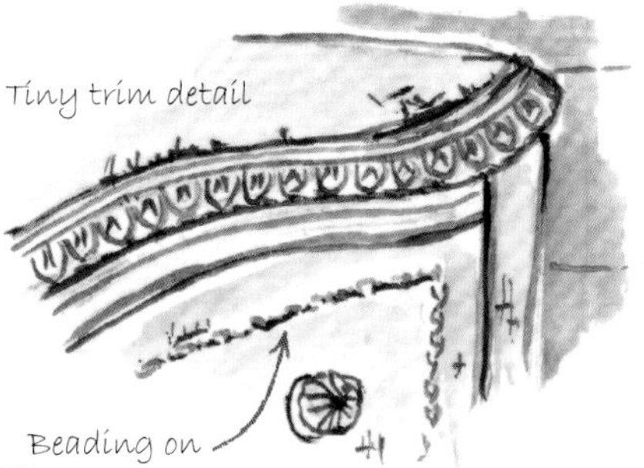

Chunky carved
roses surround
the oval mirror
elegantly braced
to pivot

Subtle kidney shape frame

Tiny trim detail

Beading on
drawers

Barley twist legs

Hand-carved roses

Mellow brass knobs

Ribbons and wreath

MARIE ANTOINETTE

I pondered how she landed up in a flea market. At what point was she no longer suited or needed in her likely grand home. Her exquisite abundant hand carvings of roses and wreaths are priceless.

Rare oval topped mirror safely set between two banks of drawers

Gentle embellishments

THE QUEEN

Sometimes even if the time isn't right, you just have to say yes, knowing it's too good a treasure to pass up. I bought this with nowhere to put her at the time. But I knew once I had the perfect space, I would regret not having her. She is a perfect example of beauty and function. Probably from the early 1900s. I'm sure she will one day find a home that matches her qualities.

Elegantly shaped
cabinetry

Fanciful carved legs

THE STAR OF THE SHOW

Aging gracefully, the console is faded in just the right places
so that now, in all her glory, she can be placed without
overpowering the space. Hand-painted gloriously turquoise,
inserted with cream panels to pronounce playful flowers.
Wonderful proportions.

Velvet cushion over grass woven seat

LONESOME CHAIR

This chair may have been
separated from her family
but special, nonetheless.

PRECIOUS & PETITE

There is something all the more special about fanciful details on small-scale pieces. Perhaps because they take up less room, they don't hold the importance of something grand. But whether for nightstands or just any little table, I always appreciate every little embellishment, carving, and accent. I'm just as happy to find pairs of small cabinets as I am to mix and match. Just bear in mind, especially for bedside tables, to try to have them the same height if you are working with matching lamps, so that they can line up.

MY "FOREVER-TO-KEEP"
She has graced many pages of my books. I love her so, so much. She is "Shabby Chic." Her simple lines balance her fanciful decoration, top and front.

Tapered legs

Caster wheels

FRENCH BLUE
Simple scroll, simple blue and white patina. Perfection even without legs.

SHABBY & CHIC

My concept of Shabby Chic was to embrace the fancy life but to welcome shabby imperfections.

Chic, intricately carved feminine pieces, with an element of formality are less intimidating and more easily placed due to their vulnerability by way of being tattered around the edges.

QUIETLY GRACEFUL
A rare find, for a coffee table or at the end of a bed, all the rarer painted in duck egg blue.

DELICATE DETAILS

Delicate hardware

Hidden tray

Sweeping slender carved legs

TIMEWORN ELEGANCE

Tall slender legs

Shabby and chic carving

THE PERFECT PINK BENCH
Sometimes small and quiet accent pieces
command center stage even though they
don't search for the limelight.

Nail heads

Velvet tufted bench and arm rests

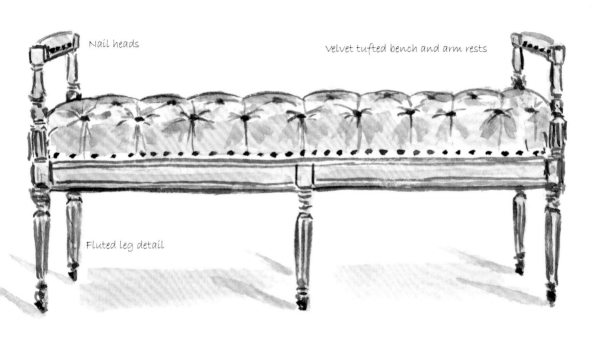

Fluted leg detail

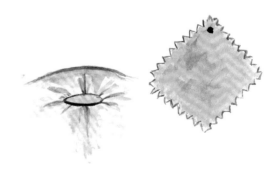

a place to dream

Bedrooms are our sanctuary. They should evoke tranquility, calm, warmth, and beauty. It's where we greet each new day and close the day we leave behind. I find great value in simplicity of the room where we sleep. Subdued lighting and little distractions, our beds are our sacred safe place. Many beautiful vintage beds have passed through my hands along with ones I that have designed. I consider the bed in which we sleep one of the most considered and valuable possessions (along with a good mattress, beautiful bedding, and comfy pillows).

Enya is one of my favorite artists to dream along to. The music and lyrics to "Dreams Are More Precious" are music to my ears and beauty to my soul.

PAINTED BEAUTY
A beautiful balance of faded grandeur by way of traditional frame with gold carved posts, decorated with whimsical faded flowers.

"Put your thoughts to sleep. Do not let them cast a shadow over the moon of your heart."

Rumi

PRECIOUS DREAMS
A classic Shabby Chic vintage bed, painted cream with elegant floral embellishments along with panels of wicker (if the wicker is broken on your bed you could get it repaired or replace with upholstered fabric panels).

It's dressed in an abundance of pillows and duvets from my ruffled blush Petticoat Collection. I designed this collection wanting to create a beautiful fantasy world to soothe the soul and just float away in peaceful thoughts.

THE FRENCH LADY
By day a settee to daydream, by night where thoughts can rest.

Collection of needlepoint pillows

Jacquard silk upholstery

Muted colors so not too sweet

Dreams are illustrations painted while we sleep.

THE LEADING LADY
A classic French bed upholstered to star quality
by way of pink velvet tufting.

HIS & HER BEDS
I love how these are nearly twins and can co-exist
side by side with just subtle differences.

Taupe-gray painted
frames with white
peeking through

HEAVENLY HANDSOME
Salvaged architectural panels can be transformed into a breathtaking headboard. Monumental elements, once just a portion of an installation, become a stand-alone spectacular backdrop for sumptuous bedding and create the place where dreams are made.

THE ONE THAT GOT AWAY
On a rare occasion I regret not keeping a treasure once found, not fully appreciating how special the treasure is until she's gone.

I loved the bold painterly flowers and the denim blue swishes of paint on a stage of neutral non-yellowing ivory.

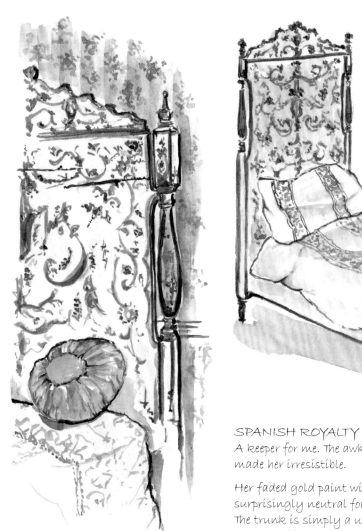

Tall slender back

Spindles

SPANISH ROYALTY
A keeper for me. The awkward proportions of this bed made her irresistible.

Her faded gold paint with turquoise accents is surprisingly neutral for easy placing in my home. The trunk is simply a useful beauty. I ponder what was stored in her, back in her heyday.

FLORAL SLEEPING ROOM

The hodgepodge of vintage treasures is placed with symmetry so that the feeling of a peaceful sanctuary remains. The silk embroidered bedcover, painting, floral painted nightstands, and floral ironwork of the lamps are romantic, but not overly fussy due to the mellow and faded palette.

cast of characters

The beauty of combining vintage treasures is the common thread of tattered elegance. As long as they are beautiful they will bring out the best in each other.

Teal velvet replaces damask on worse for wear sides and arm pads, complementing well what remains

Tufting

Mellow nail heads

Delicate carving

ROYAL DINING
Left as found, this crowning seat in neutral velvet pile damask. Originally part of a set of six but can easily hold court as one.

TRUE BLUE
Woven damask, her low-slung pitch gives a laid-back attitude.

Weathered gold carved frame

PRINCESS
She waits, quietly confident that she is irresistible. Newly upholstered in signature pink dry cotton velvet.

HANDSOME BEAUTY
Handsome in form with stately arms. Original fabric, the blue stripe balances the sweet flowers.

FORMAL FANCY
Formal and bright, diffused with floppy subdued pillows.
Its legacy was probably from a traditional home, but would
blend into a boho or eclectic space comfortably.

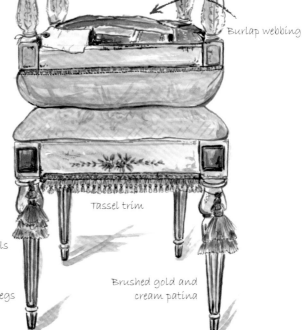

Burlap webbing

FANCY FOOTSTOOL
I like to place little accents of exquisite
moments. Not an overpowering
statement but a pause of wonderment
at the intricacy of so much beauty in
something so small.

Tassel trim

Fanciful tassels

Fluted tapered legs

Brushed gold and
cream patina

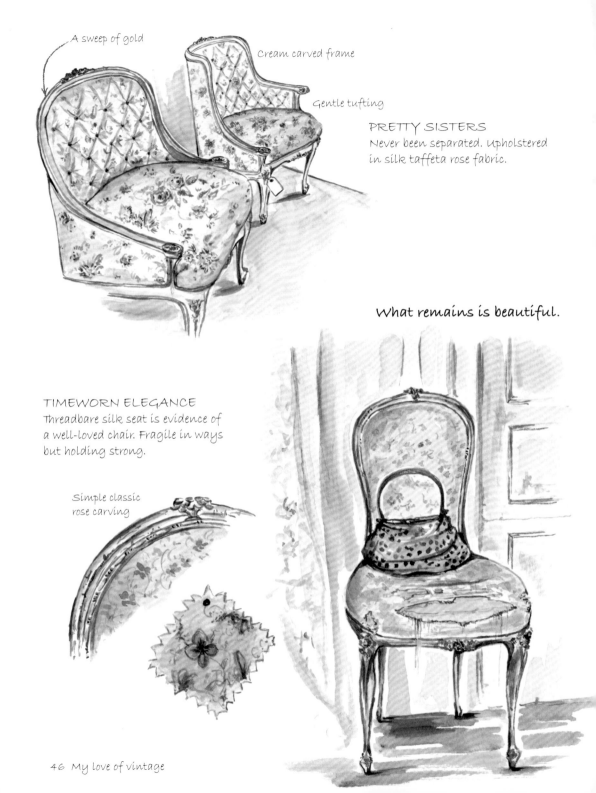

A sweep of gold

Cream carved frame

Gentle tufting

PRETTY SISTERS
Never been separated. Upholstered
in silk taffeta rose fabric.

What remains is beautiful.

TIMEWORN ELEGANCE
Threadbare silk seat is evidence of
a well-loved chair. Fragile in ways
but holding strong.

Simple classic
rose carving

GRACEFUL
A delicate gold frame and details support generous seating. Reupholstered in plush blush pink velvet.

Needlepoint pillow

FADED GRANDEUR
A threadbare back requires some acceptance that things cannot always be fully restored to how they once were, but here enough value remains to make good with oval tapestry placed front and center. In some way, it makes it all the more special.

Tapestry

Padded arm inserts

Original upholstery

LITTLE CHAIR
Dainty as can be. Sat upon more than intended, the added seat cushion provides protection for the barely-there upholstered seat.

Sometimes things are just meant to be together, without thought. And together they bring out the best in each other. And beauty is made.

Caster wheels

FLORAL ROCK'N'ROLL
The perfect clash. Classic chair, low seated in faded pink velvet and a vibrant splash of violet blue flowers, adding a moment of rock'n'roll with the leopard print throw. The ideal scale for almost any room.

Mother-of-pearl inset floral décor

THE PERFECT RHAPSODY
Rock'n'roll meets fancy serene. The balance combined is magical, paired
with what might otherwise be a serious Victorian table.

WONDERFUL WICKER

Out of Africa is one of my favorite movies where wicker galore graces the gardens and porches, creating romance and whimsy. However, wicker furniture can be a beautiful addition indoors as well. Often, it needs a fresh coat of paint or a sealer due to a life of weathering the outdoor elements. But along with freshly made mushy cushions (crisp white denim or floral vintage fabric complements well), it can receive a whole new lease on life. Do be mindful when buying if the wicker is damaged from unravelling or holes. While there are still some wicker restorers and evidence of repair can be charming, it can become costly to do so.

A piece of glass on a table can give some extra durability while still revealing the timeworn beauty of the surface. While a matching set is lovely, single wicker chairs can be found quite affordably, which makes gathering and mixing and matching worthwhile.

TIMELESS TEATIME

Glass over wicker top

Floral cushion

Stripe cushion

SEATING FOR SEVEN
Long ticking cushion. It may have been more sensible to make three cushions, but I thought one long one was a spectacular detail.

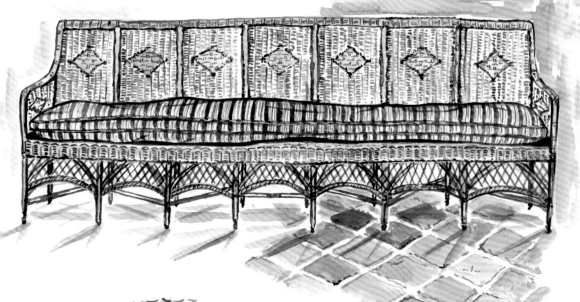

Wicker repair

FANCY & FEMININE
She's just so lovely in scale with curly scrolls.

BITS & PIECES

Finding those little pieces that just fit, when nothing else does, is always a joyful discovery.

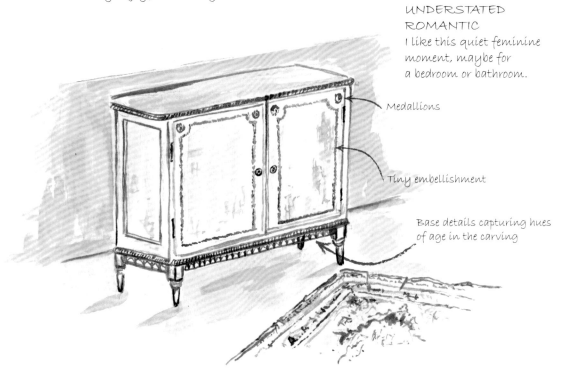

**UNDERSTATED
ROMANTIC**
I like this quiet feminine moment, maybe for a bedroom or bathroom.

Medallions

Tiny embellishment

Base details capturing hues of age in the carving

Playful floral hand-painted metal bin

RUBBISH BINS
Beauty should occur in unexpected places, creating a poetic pause for appreciation.

Pink wicker

Combination of wicker weaves

FANCY METAL

Petite tables with decorative metalwork are charming accents. They can be a little tarnished or rusty if they have lived outside in a prior chapter of their lives, but I find the often airy and intricate designs made possible by metal to be an unobtrusive layer of décor. A nice affordable detail is to replace glass with a bevel edge.

THE ANYWHERE TABLE

She's pretty and easy to move around as needed. Her frame is Moroccan, but her paint finish is pure shabby.

UNPRETENTIOUS

Unassuming, little, stocky, square, off-white painted, shabby table. Yet so very useful!

MAGICAL RUGS

Magical carpets in fairy stories, fables, and folklore symbolize carrying us away to our dreams, supporting us to soar above troubles and obstacles. Metaphorically they symbolize having an awareness that allows us to perceive life from a higher and purer point of view.

Handmade vintage carpets carry an energy different to other vintage treasures. They are like a song; they have a cadence and rhythm. Having taken months to make, they require a specific skill set and patience. Rug makers include their emotion and thoughts during the designing and creating process. Hence the colors and symbols are a language woven into the rug. Often, we do not know the intent of the message or the imagination or the surroundings of the weaver, so we are left with our intuition to choose a rug that has a good feeling as well as its beauty.

And while our homes are not fairy stories, a rug is a confined sacred space which cushions us from the floor beneath us, providing comfort and warmth.

oushak rugs

Woven in western Turkey. They evoke peace and calmness in a room. Originally produced by Nomads in the 15th century, Oushaks became significant productions in the 17th century. The craftsmen were as much concerned with the quality as the aesthetic appeal.

The density of the hand knots is most critical, as loose knots create a flimsier and less durable rug. Typically, the backgrounds are golden or ivory with faded floral or geometric designs, and when dyed with vegetable dyes the wool takes on a silky hue. Oushaks are one of my favorite constructions. I actually prefer them more flimsy than stiff for ease of layering.

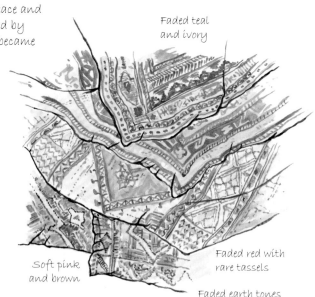

Faded teal and ivory

Soft pink and brown

Faded red with rare tassels

Faded earth tones

My favorites have ivory backgrounds which perfectly complement my signature palette of pale pinks to raspberry and baby blue to teal. Sometimes there are playful random sections of vibrant colors like raspberry nestled into paler shades of pink, making me wonder if there was a shortage of thread needed to complete the rug.

OMBRÉ DAMASK
Hand tufted cut pile.

Subtle palette of pink and brown

All-over scattered damask

HAND-HOOKED FLOWERS
Hand-hooked circular rug. Originally considered a country craft, the designs are more simplistic floral forms, by nature of the construction not overly sweet.

TODAY'S TREASURE
Replicated vintage rugs, machine made.

Rectangle

Prayer mat

Runner

runners, rugs, and prayer mats

I prefer rugs over wall-to-wall carpet. If floors are made from attractive wood, tiles, or cement in a more modern environment, multiple rugs in a space create an eclectic warmth. If wall-to-wall covering is needed, sea grass is a neutral base to layer magical rugs over.

Oushak runners can be the most affordable size of these rugs due to their limited usage. They do, however, work perfectly as an ensemble when layering in a room. I prefer to have multiple rugs placed in a room rather than one big one. They are easy to place, move around, and clean. I also like the diversity of color and design as a stage to place furniture.

Prayer mats are wonderfully placeable, affordable, and whimsical. Due to their small scale the design work appears more detailed, and the colors are often lovely within the Shabby Chic palette. I place in my bathrooms, inside my entryway, and in guest bedrooms.

If threads become bare, make little distinct, contrasting, and proud patches of acceptance of the vulnerability and imperfection. Perhaps in a bold flowery linen and apply with large whip stitches. Shine a spotlight of intentional restoration for continued loving.

Traditional rug weavers use color to convey their message and meanings woven into these treasures.

RUG COLOR MEANINGS

GREEN—Hope, spring, paradise, renewal

RED—Happiness, cheerfulness, attraction, strength, fate

BROWN—Fertility

BLUE/INDIGO—Wisdom, strength, self-mastery

YELLOW—Power, sun, glory

ORANGE—Loyalty, humility

WHITE—Purity, peace

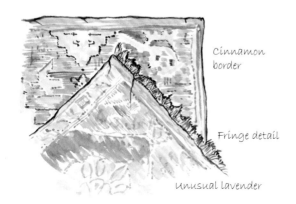

Cinnamon border

Fringe detail

Unusual lavender

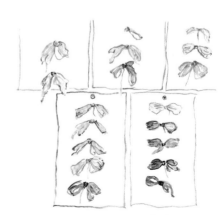

FLAT & FABULOUS

I loved this rug, just because. She has no age to her, no regarded
quality, but her colors are just dreamy. Her flat pile is lovely and
easy to keep clean. And she belongs, just for who she is.

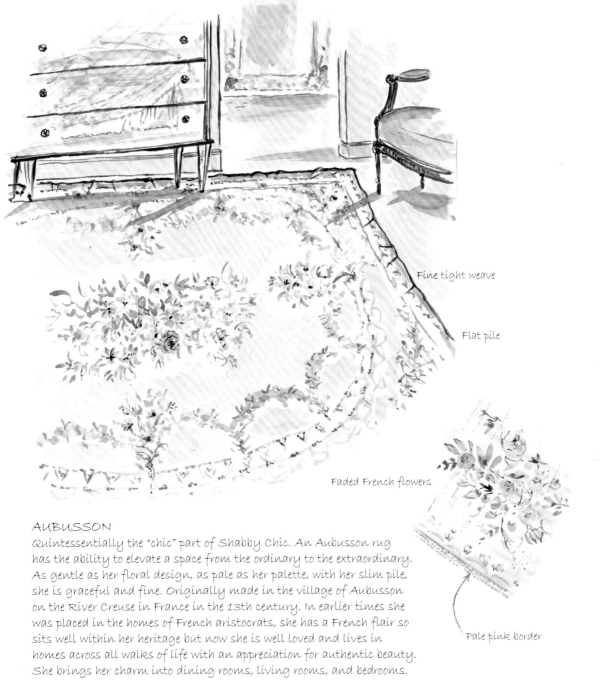

Fine tight weave

Flat pile

Faded French flowers

Pale pink border

AUBUSSON

Quintessentially the "chic" part of Shabby Chic. An Aubusson rug
has the ability to elevate a space from the ordinary to the extraordinary.
As gentle as her floral design, as pale as her palette, with her slim pile,
she is graceful and fine. Originally made in the village of Aubusson
on the River Creuse in France in the 13th century. In earlier times she
was placed in the homes of French aristocrats, she has a French flair so
sits well within her heritage but now she is well loved and lives in
homes across all walks of life with an appreciation for authentic beauty.
She brings her charm into dining rooms, living rooms, and bedrooms.

Most Aubussons made after 1870 are now replicated in China or India,
maintaining the fine signature qualities.

TWINKLING LIGHTS

When I first cast the characters in my world of Shabby Chic, my vision was to create a world of soulful simplicity with nostalgic glamour for the home. A timeworn flaky stool sharing space with a heavily laden crystal chandelier perfectly creates the harmony of my vision. It's as though the shabby little stool gives the fancy chandelier some humility and the chandelier validates the value of the sometimes-forgotten stool.

Lighting has the ability to create an ethereal veil in a home, whether by way of being front and center or a moment of beauty in an unexpected place.

It's only on a rare occasion that I buy newly-made light fixtures. I find that the whimsy, intricate details, quality, and patina of wood and metals of eclectic vintage options bring a uniqueness into the home.

As with all vintage shopping, searching for lighting is an art of patience. But I would rather live without than substitute and settle for mediocrity.

CRÈME DE LA CRÈME
She is just glorious with her graceful eight arms.
Topped with pleated silk ruffled wonky shades.

THE QUARTET

Vintage lighting creates an ambience of twinkles and whimsy that is timeless.

Hidden little details collectively create light pieces that are quietly substantive.

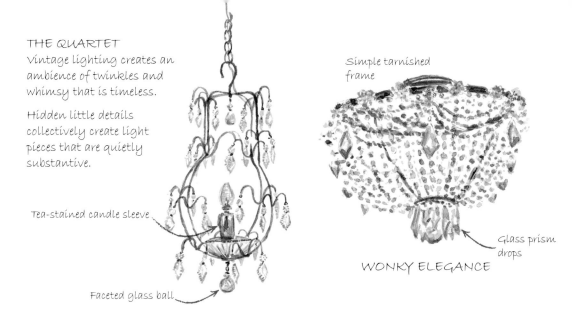

Simple tarnished frame

Tea-stained candle sleeve

Glass prism drops

Faceted glass ball

WONKY ELEGANCE

CLEARANCE FOR HANGING CHANDELIERS
7ft (2.13m) from the base to the ground
3½ft (1.07m) from base to table
5ft (1.52m) from base to mattress

QUIET UNDERSTUDY

Flared, fluted, and frosted. While the shade is important, she is nothing without the perfectly timeworn socket and chain. Perfect for bathroom or in multiples for kitchen or hallway.

PENELOPE JEWELRY CHANDELIER

The negative space between the glass beads creates an openness while still feeling abundant with beading. I designed her, inspired by a vintage find.

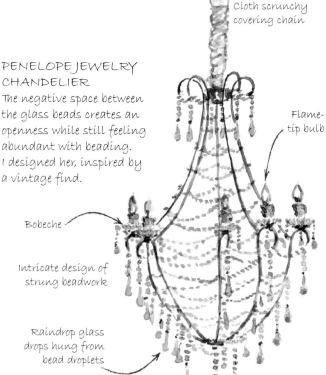

Cloth scrunchy covering chain

Flame-tip bulb

Bobeche

Intricate design of strung beadwork

Raindrop glass drops hung from bead droplets

Clear electrical cord

Vintage socket

Vintage tarnished chain

Glass shade (new or vintage easily found)

Glass rosettes

RAINBOW SPRINKLES

An elegant chandelier with a gypsy spirit shown in her boho rainbow of glass crystal drops.

Clear glass crystals reflect light and shadows, colored glass adds a tint and glow.

When I designed the restaurant Madre's for Jennifer Lopez, she requested that all the chandeliers have amber-colored drops due to their flattering glow.

Faceted colorful almond drops

Filament flame tip bulbs

Cut glass finial

Rosette

PURPLE DROP TABLE LIGHT

The offspring of the rainbow chandelier is this statuesque lamp. One of my favorites. Continuing the legacy of glass crystal drops.

Purple is one of the more common (but still so special) shades of vintage glass crystal drops. A little bit handsome and a little bit beautiful.

Purple faceted almond drops

Brown cloth cord

TRUE BLUE TEARDROPS
She's simply lovely and has lived in
my boudoir for many years.

Rosette

Feminine form

Mellow tarnished chain
(patina very important,
avoid bright gold)

Pleated ivory
silk shades

Tiny glass
beads

Blue teardrops

Wax drop candle sleeves

Delicate rippled
glass bobeche

PRETTY IN PINK

Raspberry pink tear drops

hidden details

Chandeliers are intricate and complex. Many tiny details contribute to their overall grace.

There are many sources for spare parts if you find yourself with an incomplete treasure.

Sometimes the glass beads from which the crystal glass drops hang are smooth and sometimes they are shapes with edges, such as octagons. For me it's the rings that string the beads together that create the beauty of how they drape.

Vintage beading is joined with tiny rings, often with gentle signs of aging. Newer chandeliers often have large rings which I find unsightly and take away from the grace of the drape.

Sometimes the frame of a chandelier is wrapped with tiny beads by hand, imperfectly perfect. This is a cherished detail. The application of strips of beads onto the frame of new chandeliers is too uniformed for my liking. Sometimes vintage toile frames have pretty applied décor of leaves or florals.

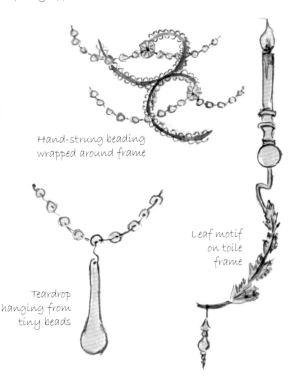

Hand-strung beading wrapped around frame

Leaf motif on toile frame

Teardrop hanging from tiny beads

A scrunchy is a good solution to covering excessive chain. However I do like an exposed mellow chain if it's a short installation.

Scrunchy

Beaded bulb cover

Bobeche tiny beads

Tiny chain

Crystal ball

SHAPES OF CRYSTAL PENDALOGUES AND DROPS

Rosettes (usually used for attaching strings of beads to drops)

Pear shape (clear or faceted)

Almond shape (clear or faceted)

Icicle

Crystal cut center balls (clear or faceted)

Hexagon drops

Teardrop (my favorite)

Teardrop glass hanging from drapes of tiny beads joined with little rings

Bobeche

Clear glass ball

grand majesty

Twinkling and casting a magical shadow. Quintessentially Shabby.

A chandelier has an emotional quality to her beauty. She represents romance and timeless characteristics. Once placed she will be forever adored, like a forever love.

The shape, scale, glass crystals, and design of how the beads are strung are the components that set the tone and attitude of a chandelier. While there is a vast choice to choose from, the fundamental common thread is how they all come together, in harmony.

The word chandelier originated from the French word "chandelle," meaning candle, which chandeliers originally held.

Crystal chandeliers are mostly made from glass. True crystal drops have a lead content, are heavier and scratch more easily, but their brightness is more brilliant.

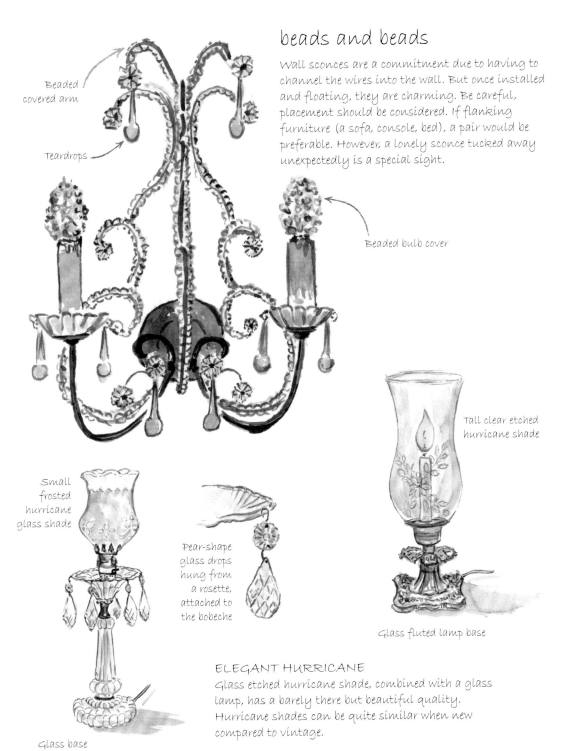

beads and beads

Wall sconces are a commitment due to having to channel the wires into the wall. But once installed and floating, they are charming. Be careful, placement should be considered. If flanking furniture (a sofa, console, bed), a pair would be preferable. However, a lonely sconce tucked away unexpectedly is a special sight.

Beaded covered arm

Teardrops

Beaded bulb cover

Tall clear etched hurricane shade

Small frosted hurricane glass shade

Pear-shape glass drops hung from a rosette, attached to the bobeche

Glass fluted lamp base

ELEGANT HURRICANE

Glass etched hurricane shade, combined with a glass lamp, has a barely there but beautiful quality. Hurricane shades can be quite similar when new compared to vintage.

Glass base

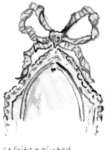

CHANDELIER TABLE LIGHT
As impactful as a hanging chandelier,
a table lamp is lovely, too.

Floral chintz
shades

White painted
metal with delicate
ribbon detail

Whimsically
sprinkled glass
drops

SINGULAR BEAUTY
Maybe was always single, maybe
she has been separated. But she's
an easily placed treasure.

Worn brass base

LOW SLUNG ELEGANCE
Harmony of palette.

Dusty pink pleated
and tasselled silk
shades

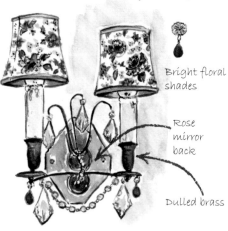

Bright floral
shades

Rose
mirror
back

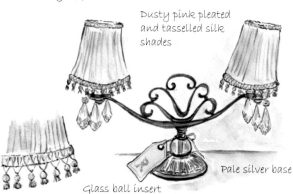

Dulled brass

Pale silver base

Glass ball insert

TURQUOISE TREAT
Love, love, love this. The perfect symphony of synchronicity.

Worn cardboard wax
candle sleeves

Unobtrusive frame

Petal
bobeches

Opaque turquoise
miniature teardrops

Gracefully strung
beads

Twinkling lights 69

accent choices

Even if a light fixture appears to be in working order, I advise having it checked by a licensed electrician.

There are also a few details that can complete the beauty of your found lighting treasure, all easily found at lighting supply stores or online.

Flame-tip lightbulbs. Clear revealing filament, slender or full.

When rewiring, choose either clear plastic, or white, or brown cord.

Bobeches—if your chandelier doesn't come with any, they are a lovely addition to slide over candle sleeve of lamp or chandelier.

Candle sleeves—I love white plastic or cardboard with wax drips.

Aged brass vintage lamp switch.

Bulb clip. Easy solution to support a shade on the lamp.

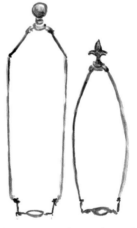

Harps come in various sizes. The shade sits on the harp and should just cover the tip of the socket.

Finials can bring a lamp fixture to life, fancily or simply. Made from dull metal (silver or gold), distressed or raw wood, or crystal (plain or decorative), finials screw into the top of the lamp to hold the harp (the component which attaches the shade to the bulb) in place.

Chandeliers need to twinkle. Every few months clean the drops. There are options of drip and dry cleaning products to spray the glass crystals with a towel under the fixture to catch the drips as it dries.

Vintage cardboard shade in a palette of gold and soft sage

standing lamps

Standing lamps are a wonderful way to create a soft spotlight on a personal space within a room.

Barely-there linen shade

SHE STANDS

HE STANDS

Faded gold fluted wood stand

Turned raw wood stand

eccentric accents

Sometimes I come across decorative lamps that are
beautiful and characterfully tell a story.

WISE OWL
Knowing that owls symbolize wisdom
and solitude, I parted company with this
handsome white owl and gave it as a gift
to my son. I added a simple oatmeal
rectangular pleated shade.

EXOTIC DANCER
I love mermaids for their mysterious
fairy-story quality. I had thought she
was a mermaid but on closer viewing
she was actually an exotic dancer.
I still felt she had a magical quality,
along with her silk tassel shade.

quirky glamour

Oversized lampshades remind me of Alice in Wonderland. And how perfectly wonderful to use them for a hanging shade in lieu of having a lampstand.

Oversized blue floral shade

Oversized pink ruffled shade

lace to dry

Tea staining or dyeing found lampshades is an easily accomplished and satisfying solution to transforming a treasure to a palette of choice.

Lace shades dipped in dye and drying

little big lamps

They may be small but make for a meaningful moment. For a guest room, a little girl's room, or when in need of a special frilly moment.

These little vintage charms always amaze me with their exquisite attention to detail. There is such beauty in their modesty. I appreciate every little flower, ruffle, and sparkle.

FEATHERY FRILLS

"If you light a lamp for someone else it will also brighten your path."

Buddha

Slender glass stem

Delicate porcelain flowers

Heavy glass base

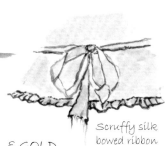

Scruffy silk bowed ribbon

PASTEL & GOLD

TUTU SHADE

Plastic but pretty pale blue with a lace effect shade

Tiny velvet flower and ribbon

Nicely shaped porcelain base with decal roses

Pale blue shade

Pale gold stem

Pale pink base

FLUFFY RUFFLE

Cream shade sandwiched with a fluffy ruffle

Rose embroidered ribbon

Pop of blue

Hobnail glass base

ALL ABOUT THE SHADE

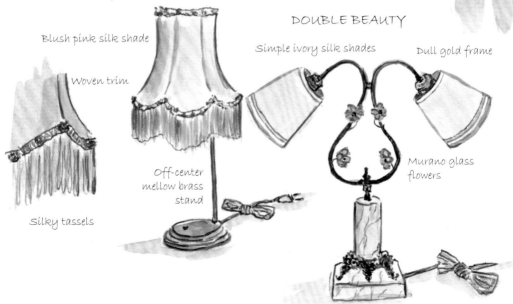

Blush pink silk shade

Woven trim

Silky tassels

Off-center mellow brass stand

DOUBLE BEAUTY

Simple ivory silk shades

Dull gold frame

Murano glass flowers

White marble base

alabaster

Marble and alabaster vintage bases are a neutral beauty. They can be dressed up fancily or they are handsome enough to be paired with a simple, fresh white linen shade.

FEMININE & SHAPELY

Harp awaiting shade

Simple dusty pink linen shade

HANDSOMELY CARVED

Subtle carving

shades on top

Sometimes I buy bases without shades, and sometimes I buy shades without bases.

Pretty lampshades are treasures when found, kept safe until their perfect partner comes along. And when she does it's like they were always meant for each other.

Silk shade with trim applied by hand

Pale blue velvet ribbon, stitched in place by hand

Plastic lace effect

chapter 3

WHIMSICAL ACCENTS

Furniture is the anchor in our homes and the pieces command attention by the nature of their size. They come to life with whimsical accessories.

When I shop at flea markets and antique shops, it's as though I have two sets of eyes, simultaneously seeking and editing. One set is searching for furniture that is more easily spotted, while at the same time I hone in on the smaller treasures. It's a matter of training your eyes and following your instincts, you know what you love. And lastly, it's important to have patience. A void of nothing is better than buying the wrong thing. Never settle for mediocrity. There are enough wonderful treasures to be found when the time is right and the stars align.

I believe every detail in the home is part of our story. It's never-ending as we evolve. Our story is forever changing, and we often outgrow what once served a purpose. The smaller treasures are like the punctuation marks in our visual memoirs so they must be chosen mindfully. There is a plethora of choice with varied aesthetics and functions, but the magic happens when we create our authentic story and our house becomes a home.

"Thousands of candles can be lighted from a single candle, and the life of the candle will not be shortened. Happiness never decreases by being shared."

Buddha

DELIGHTFUL DINING WITH BEST CHINA

I strongly believe, whether for a snack or a feast, our best china should be used every day and celebrated.

I have a mismatched assortment of plates, cups, glasses, and serving dishes that I have collected on my travels. Some are fine French Limoges porcelain and some are unmarked but they are equally valuable to me. I don't own any complete sets of china as I prefer mixing and matching, it's less intimidating and less formal. I also think it is more personal to layer pieces from all walks of life and let them come together beautifully with equal value. As an added plus, buying individual pieces is more affordable. If little nicks and cracks happen along the way I move them along to other duties, like perhaps using them as a vase, so rarely do they need to be discarded completely. But if something does get broken beyond repair, the knowledge that there are more mismatched beauties to be found gives me the freedom to enjoy these fragile and precious beauties every day.

Many years ago, I designed the restaurant Madre's, for Jennifer Lopez. We wanted to use unique and beautiful vintage china. But with the practicality of washing large quantities of dishes in mind we layered everyday white dinnerware along with the vintage pieces, which worked well to help create a pause of specialness amongst plain and simple.

PINK FLORAL

Raspberry embroidered table runner and napkin

Fine embossed silver cutlery

No day in life is a dress rehearsal so every
day is worthy of our best china.

truly amazing

I never cease to be amazed at the intricacies, in both the
shape and the often hand-painted artistry in many of the
pieces I find. Always wondering how and why they ended
up being discarded. But that's the beauty of having the
insight and thought to bring something back from
oblivion and give it new purpose, validating its
value because you see something special.

TUMBLER TREAT
Cut glass tumbler with
gold highlights

Turquoise scattered petals

Mother-of-pearl cutlery

Crown embroidered
linen napkin

SIMPLY REGAL

SAUCERLESS CUP
Too beautiful to discard, with raised blue ribbon
effect and gold trim (I use it to keep my rings
nestled safely inside).

FRIENDS
ARE
LIKE
FLOWERS
In the
garden of life

TOO TRUE

happy hodgepodge

Although I usually drink tea continuously throughout the day, teatime (around 3.30-4pm) is a sacred ritual for me. It gives me pause to reflect on the day and a boost of energy for the time that remains.

I also love to host a proper teatime occasion, for one friend or many. I like the formality of precious china, with all its fancy and glory, enjoyed informally.

VASE

FANCY LITTLE
SUGAR BOWL LID

Fancy handles

Oversized flowers

Ruffled base

SUGAR BOWL

FRILLY TEA FOR FOUR
Lovely décor and shape.

A VARIETY OF TEA TIMES

Elevenses: Mid-morning tea break (usually around 11am).

Cream tea: Tea with scones, clotted cream, and jam.

Low tea: Served in the afternoon, tea with small sandwiches, scones, and cream. Called low tea because guests were served in low armchairs with low side tables.

Royal tea: Same as low tea, but accompanied with a glass of Champagne or sherry.

High tea: What we might now know as supper or dinner, called high tea as it was served at a table. Historically, upper classes developed their own variation of a high tea, that could be made and eaten quickly with ease on Sundays so their maids and butlers could go to church and not be concerned with an evening meal.

"I must drink lots of tea or I cannot work. Tea unleashes the potential which slumbers in the depth of my soul."

Leo Tolstoy

tea is served

The presentation of how tea is served is part of the simple but meaningful experience. Many a morning I have served my children breakfast in bed on the prettiest little trays.

TOILE TRAYS
Floral painted toile trays from Italy.

Delicate powder blue

Perfect baby pink

TINY TEA FOR TWO
Glamorous in spite of its size.

PLATES FOR CAKE

Delicate gold rim

Scattered roses

SCENIC SUGAR BOWL WITH LID

Delightful dining with best china 83

FLATWARE

Cutlery made all the more special with the added detail of the hand stamped "LOVE YOU," whether for a wedding table or for oneself.

ETIQUETTE FROM DAYS GONE BY FOR A PROPER CUP OF TEA

1. Unfold napkin onto lap.

2. Place sugar or lemon first.

3. Pour brewed tea.

4. Lastly add milk and stir.

5. Spoon replaced on saucer.

6. Never put your pinky up.

7. Look into cup when drinking, not over it.

(And if you're lucky enough to have an English scone)

8. Split horizontally with a knife.

9. Add cream and jam as needed for each bite.

10. Eat with fingers, neatly.

TEACUP TREASURES

The first known teacups were handleless bowls, often causing scorched hands. So I think we all owe much gratitude to Robert Adams, who back in the 1700s invented porcelain teacups with handles and saucers, followed by teapots, sugar holders, and creamers.

TREASURES FOR TEA

No detail has gone astray. Delicate flowers enhanced with gold embellishments, scalloped edges. Sentimental words complement the palette.

LONESOME CUP

Lost its saucer but still it comes to the party with its rippled skirt effect beauty.

LOVELY LUSTER

One of my favorite decoration techniques on china or porcelain is created with an effect called lusterware. Pieces are decorated with metallic luster that gives them an iridescent quality. Typically, I have seen these in many shades of pink, sometimes blue.

A FEAST FOR THE EYES

I am drawn to teacups, dinnerware, and serving pieces mainly from the early 20th century through to about the 1920s. Often from France, Germany, eastern Europe, and Japan. Mostly pastel florals with some brighter raspberry and blue tones, along with fine artistry of gold designs and trims placed on bright white china. They have a gorgeousness and decadence to them, bringing a priceless addition to any table setting both formal and informal. A quintessential Shabby Chic table embraces mixing and matching colors, motifs, and shapes together, creating a visual symphony.

GRAND SERVING PLATTER

Raspberry florals with gold trim.

MATCH MADE IN HEAVEN

Layering this pink floral bread plate with a teal floral dinner plate creates a wonderful pairing.

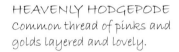

HEAVENLY HODGEPODE

Common thread of pinks and golds layered and lovely.

PETITE SERVING DISH

Gold medallion motif.

COUNTRY CHARM

Blue formal plate layered with treasures.

Brooch pin acting as napkin holder

Horseshoe charm

Ditsy napkin

THE MOST BEAUTIFUL BACKSTAMPS

Backstamps are symbols of authenticity of a manufacturer and are of the utmost importance for those interested in knowing the history or monetary value of a piece of porcelain, china, or pottery. I love a backstamp for the added beauty hidden away, often smudged, incomplete, or faded. I never buy anything for any other reason than I love it, and especially never for its monetary value. I find little details of inspiration in these small special marks that then become part of a bigger story.

INCOMPLETE FLORAL WREATH

CREST & CROWN

SMUDGY CROWN

CHURCH SOUVENIR
Designed in the spirit of a back stamp but proudly placed front and center on the plate.

SHABBY CHIC LOGO
Inspired by elements of many different backstamps.

THE BOTTLES
Every little detail creates the overall harmony of a table setting. If choice permits, just choose pretty.

BLUE BOY
Gin isn't my thing, but everything about this bottle is. So, it belongs.

PRETTY IN PINK

Little silver cap

Perfect shade of aqua blue

Handsome label with gold trim

Clean lines of bottle

Sweet pink lemonade

Lovely label

Feminine shape

GLORIOUS GLASSWARE

I am certain I have hosted many dinner parties where I have not supplied the "correct" complementary glasses for wine connoisseurs. I have always prioritized beauty over specific function. I love to gather beautiful glasses from all walks of life and let them group together with other beauties, of all shapes, sizes, and nationalities, and then let whatever will be will be, whether water, wine, or anything else. The common thread across everything and everyone is equal value regardless from where it came, creating a space for authenticity and beauty.

GLASS GOBLET

Whimsically would fit in at the "Mad Hatter's Tea Party" or Marie Antoinette's table.

Not fine glass but sturdy with lovely lines and pressed glass details.

Rubbed-down gold trim

RELIGIOUS PAUSE

I have a couple of these. They are made from very fine glass with very meaningful words.

Painted flowers and words

MORROCAN MOMENT

Adding a boho flair into the mix.

GRACEFUL CRYSTAL

Simple and sparkling as is the nature of crystal.

ROYALTY

Little crown

Big crown

ROSES ON ROSES

Hard for this floral cake plate to compete with the cake. But anything less lovely wouldn't complement the star with the beauty she deserves.

Scalloped roses

CANDLELIGHT

Candles radiate romance and nostalgia. A simple white drip candle contributes to bringing a layer of magic, whether placed in a fancy or simple holder. As stunning as a centerpiece on a table as they are calming on a dresser in a bedroom, their timelessness gives us comfort in the joy of the simple things of life. Metaphorically speaking, candles represent to me the acceptance of impermanence, appreciating their glow as the wax melts away.

ROMANTIC MEMORIES
I saw these in a pub. Cascading wax of many shades of romantic pink. Couldn't help but think sometimes the remains become more beautiful than the memory of what was.

Elton John sang about a candle in the wind never knowing who to cling to... Even so, something magnificent comes into being.

BRUISED BEAUTIES
My favorite pair of candlesticks. Even with chipped porcelain flowers and peeling painted white metal leaves, this pair of beautiful candlesticks hold their dignity, grace, and beauty.

Non-fragrant drippy candles

TURNED WOOD CANDLESTICKS
Simple, unpretentious purest beauty. Multiples grouped together would transform into a breathtaking statement.

GOODNIGHT
Solitary white porcelain candle holder with painted flowers. Feels like a scene from **Little Women** to me.

Metal leaves

Porcelain flowers

PERFUME FOR YOUR HOME

Fragrance is a lasting memory. Like a song, it is often an aroma that brings back memories long forgotten, often more so than a visual recollection. While I welcome many candles into my home, there are just a few distinct fragrances that are my true loves. Subtle but memorable.

DREAMY DIPTYQUE
A journey into the home.

Diptyque is a French-based haute perfumery. It is the most whimsical as well as substantive of brands. Their story telling and depth of passion into every detail are inspiring. Founded by a gypsy-esque threesome: Christian Montadre-Gautrot, an interior designer, Yves Coueslant, a theater set designer, and Desmond Knox-Leet, a painter. They introduced their first candle in 1963 from the Diptyque store at 34 Boulevard Saint-Germain in Paris, France. Their labeling, inspired by the Roman shields of the Pretorian Guard, combined with the magical journey of developing their fragrances through metaphorical as well as genuine secret gardens, brings pure soul to the candle plus an aroma that is unmatched.

Personally, I love the Baies fragrance, which is made up of notes of blackcurrant berries, along with their green leaves and a flowery accent of rose. This scent has become a trademark in my home.

PURPLE IRIS
Santa Maria Novella is a luxury apothecary in Florence, Italy.

The church of Santa Maria Novella and its monastery date back to 1221 where monks experimented with herbs and flowers, creating soothing balms and elixirs. Today the pharmacy is in an extraordinary building in Florence with vaulted ceilings, ornate gilding, frescoes, and marble floors. Walnut cabinetry houses glass decanters with colorful potions. It is truly breathtaking.

While there are many beautiful products, my personal favorite is the Iris candle, which provides a beautiful fragrance to my home altar, where my collection of vintage Virgin Marys lives. Manufactured in the Via Reginaldo Giuliani facility in Florence, its fragrance is reminiscent of the iris flower, the symbol of Florence. A divine detail of a gold-painted fleur de lis graces the front of the candle.

MY HOME ALTAR

Wherever I call home, I have my special place of prayer and meditation. To me it is my spiritual corner that represents faith, trust, and gratitude. Along with my Iris candle, a small flower, and a cross, I place a Virgin Mary. The ensemble helps me to create a meaningful pause in life. A sense of calmness that touches my soul.

THE CROSSES
I love the simplicity and artistry of crosses I have found.

FRENCH CLAY
He's quiet, he's beautiful, graced with a small denim-blue silk ribbon.

Pierced hole for nail

Gold trim

HOLY TRIO
Charming porcelain holy water plaques. Decoratively meaningful. Found at a French brocante.

ORNAMENTAL SHELL
Artfully made by hand.

TWO GENTLE SOULS
Part of my lighter shades of pale collection. Peaceful and hopeful facial expression.

As I gather religious figurines I pause to connect with their energy and to seek love in their faces. I am very selective as I feel these are very powerful and personal pieces to bring into our sanctuaries.

VIRGIN MARY & CHILD

Most of my collection of Virgin Marys are white or with a touch of pastel, made from bisque and porcelain. Often noses and fingers are rubbed down due to their vulnerability to breakages, but also I'm told it is where they are most often touched for prayer.

But even with this one's brighter palette I love her still. She has her own special place in my home and radiates faith and trust.

PRETTY PACKAGES

Presentation means the world to me, whether the present is
personally gift wrapped or is preciously boxed from the store.
Unlike not being able to tell a book by its cover, I am rarely
disappointed by the contents, knowing if the packaging is
beautiful, the inside likely is, too.

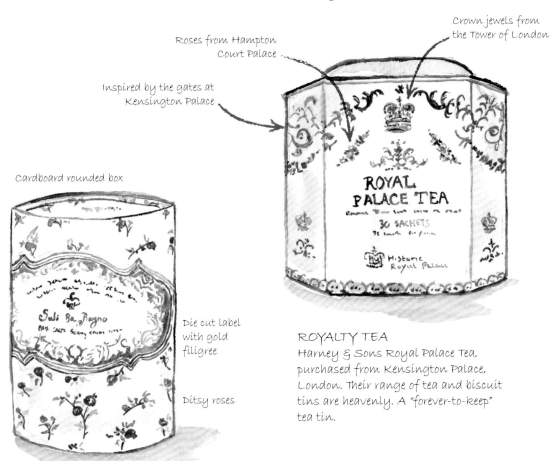

Crown jewels from
the Tower of London

Roses from Hampton
Court Palace

Inspired by the gates at
Kensington Palace

Cardboard rounded box

Die cut label
with gold
filigree

Ditsy roses

ROYALTY TEA
Harney & Sons Royal Palace Tea,
purchased from Kensington Palace,
London. Their range of tea and biscuit
tins are heavenly. A "forever-to-keep"
tea tin.

BATHING SALTS
Melograno bath salts by the beloved Santa Maria Novella.
While the bath salts themselves are like no other, made with
age-old recipes created by Dominican Friars in 1221 in
Florence, I would buy the box if empty. So charming.

A gift of beauty will be an everlasting memory in our hearts.

Tulle ruffle

Silver top

Embossed "R"

TUTU AND R
I can only imagine how lovely the scent is, worthy of being contained so beautifully in a pale pink bottle with her tulle collar.

SAINT SOAP BOX

Pale pink round handmade box

Gold lettering

PINK MARC DE CHAMPAGNE
One of my favorites to give and receive. Founded in Paris in 1875 by Madame Charbonnel and Mrs Walker, this is an exquisite double layer handmade box with iconic Pink Marc de Champagne chocolate truffles. A yummy white chocolate with a hint of strawberry and a creamy milk chocolate in the center. All rolled in a little powdered sugar for an extra touch of elegance. Simply beautiful inside and out. This was a favorite of Princess Diana's, too.

Ladurée gift box

Pale gold ribbon

Wide floppy silk ribbon

Tiffany box

"FOREVER-TO-KEEP"

Gifts to me come with feeling, often longer lasting and
memorable than the gift itself. I always keep pretty boxes
and ribbons from past gifts I have received.

Using my archive of pretty trims, floppy ribbons, and
vintage flowers, a beautifully wrapped gift comes to life,
and because created personally from the heart, it's all the
more meaningful. I find great joy in gift giving.

BEJEWELED COOKIES

PASTEL TREATS

Gift giving is all about the thought. I like to write metaphors and meanings that reflect the simplest of gifts, when putting it altogether.

For these pretty treats I might write, "You are the sweetest most beautiful friend, I value every big and little detail of who you are. We have shared all the shades of life creating a rainbow of a friendship." I would then pop these treats in a vintage box, lined with pastel tissue paper, a priceless gift for pennies.

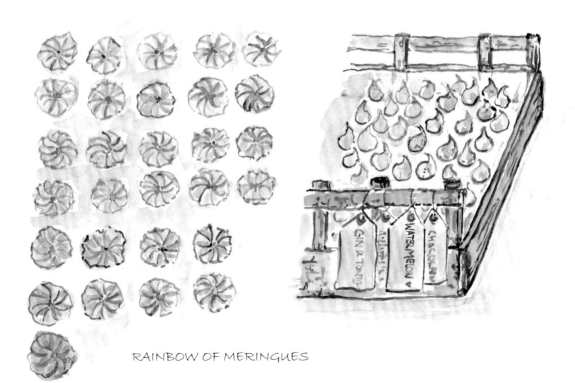

RAINBOW OF MERINGUES

RIBBONS & BOWS by Laurence Amélie

The final touch. Grand bow secured with love.

The loving thought remains a distant memory forever.

TINS FOR TREASURES

My archive of bits and bobs (ribbons, lace, buttons, floppy flowers) is kept organized and worthy of being on show in pretty tin boxes. Eye candy inside and out.

TRIO OF TINS

FLEAMARKET FOUND

My perfect palette.

Hexagonal shape

Dash of raspberry

Palest blue glass

RACHEL ASHWELL
RUBY JEWEL

RACHEL ASHWELL
MISTY MEMORYS

TRAVELING TREASURES

Ruby Jewel and Misty Memory are my travel companions. Miniature fragrances that I developed for my Rachel Ashwell brand. Just humble little tins to take on the road, of calming soulful aromas to infuse wherever I may go.

PASTEL HOLIDAY

Even for holiday décor I remain true to my palette. I am not a
fan of red, green, and orange, so over the years I have designed
and gathered holiday décor in my preferred colors of pale pink,
baby blue, silver, and gold.

DUSTY BLUE

BLUSH

Floppy flower

Lacy dyed
ribbon

PALE GOLD

White paper wreath of roses

PUMPKINS
While I love real
off-white pumpkins, when
created in gentle shades of
velvet they are dreamy and tie
into Shabby Chic décor perfectly.

PRETTY LITTLE PATCHES
Meaningful words and sayings say so much.

I collect them in all shapes to include with a gift,
or be the gift itself.

TEENY TINY

Embroidered crest shape patches.

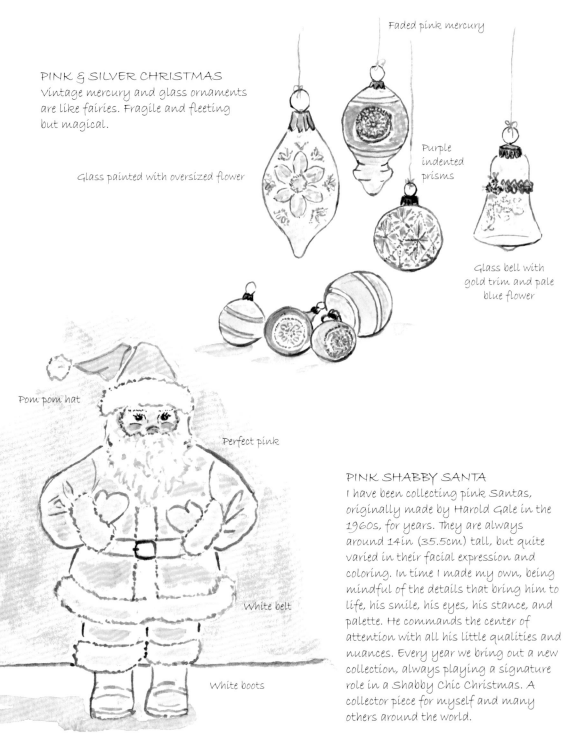

PINK & SILVER CHRISTMAS
Vintage mercury and glass ornaments are like fairies. Fragile and fleeting but magical.

Faded pink mercury

Glass painted with oversized flower

Purple indented prisms

Glass bell with gold trim and pale blue flower

Pom pom hat

Perfect pink

White belt

White boots

PINK SHABBY SANTA
I have been collecting pink Santas, originally made by Harold Gale in the 1960s, for years. They are always around 14in (35.5cm) tall, but quite varied in their facial expression and coloring. In time I made my own, being mindful of the details that bring him to life, his smile, his eyes, his stance, and palette. He commands the center of attention with all his little qualities and nuances. Every year we bring out a new collection, always playing a signature role in a Shabby Chic Christmas. A collector piece for myself and many others around the world.

PRETTY PAPER THINGS
Faded tissue and crepe paper have an ethereal feel. Both so fragile as they gently fade and mottle.

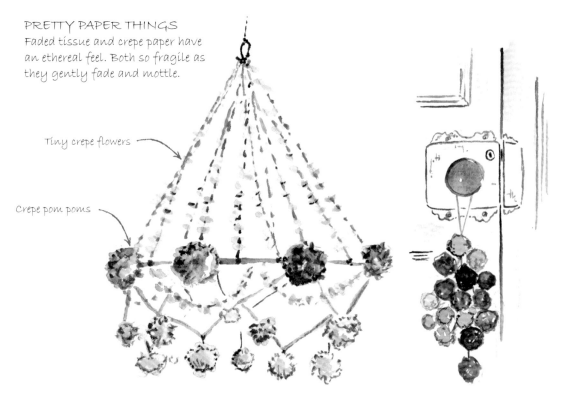

Tiny crepe flowers

Crepe pom poms

CREPE CHANDELIER
While not functional for light, its function is to bring a moment of beauty.

CLUSTERED CREPE BALLS

TISSUE BELLS
While white tissue bells are often used for weddings, other shades and sizes are a whimsical touch for gift wrap or décor. This one's delicacy brings a layer of beauty that is easily placed. I have a couple on my mood boards and tiny ones hanging from an armoire.

THE LOOKING GLASS

In Greek mythology, Narcissus fell in love with his own reflection in a still lake as he went to quench his thirst. But each time he leaned in to kiss his reflection it disappeared. Out of fear of losing his reflection he didn't dare to disturb the water or leave the lake, and eventually he died of thirst.

Thankfully by the Renaissance period in Europe, mirrors were developed by coating glass with tin and mercury amalgam. By the 16th century Venice began manufacturing these mirrors with ornate decorative frames (to this day Venetian mirrors are my favorite).

Mirrors have long inspired fairy tales and storytelling. I loved reading Lewis Carroll's twisted reality, **Through the Looking-Glass, and What Alice Found There**, where Alice enters a fantastical world by climbing through a mirror. Here, everything is reversed, like a reflection.

In **Snow White**, the mirror is a mystical object. It refracts what we believe is reality, when actually it's just an inverted mirage. In truth, it's our own interpretations that determine "who is the fairest of them all."

In Roman mythology, the breaking of a mirror causes seven years of bad luck, based on the theory that the soul shatters with the broken mirror and it takes seven years for the soul to regenerate.

Today mirrors have a magical and beautiful quality that is a mainstay in home décor, whether as a statement feature, or tucked away, only occasionally caught by a sideways glance. Along with a mirror's practical function, it can also give an illusion of expanding the size of a space, as well as adding splendor and romance using an array of decorative frames.

When everything in a home is beautiful, so too will be the reflection.

DREAMS REFLECTED
Large Italian Venetian mirror.

This fine treasure may have lived in
a fanciful home in days gone by.
She has aged gracefully with just
a little mottling on her mirror, so
her magnificance remains. She
keeps the integrity of her timeless
classic beauty and blends into
a modern aesthetic wonderfully.

Rounded etched mirror

Pastel glass rosettes

PRINCESS MIRROR
Ornate, timeless, a little bit Shabby, a lot Chic.

I probably would have been intimidated by her in her
heyday. But with her edges being a little tattered she
has an air of welcoming humility. All the more ethereal
with candle holders framing the oval mirror.

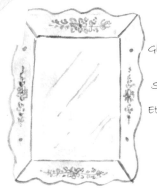

Glass nail heads

Scalloped edges

Etching

SWEET & SIMPLE
I love a simple Venetian mirror with her understated details still commanding quite the presence.

Original chain

Floral etching

MODESTY MIRROR
On first glance there may seem little to the eye, but it has quite the sparkle from the scalloped bevel edges.

Scalloped bevel

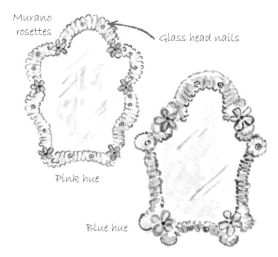

Center crest with floral embellishment

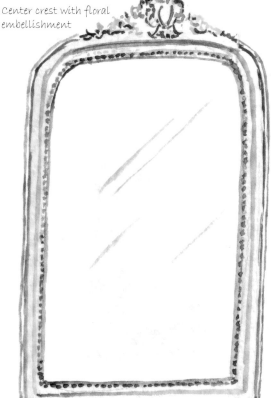

Beaded surround

Murano rosettes

Glass head nails

Pink hue

Blue hue

ROMANTIC REFLECTION
Evidence of gold under white. A few nicks and chips of faded glamour.

VENETIAN GLASS DELICACY
Exuding opulence beyond its small size. From boudoir to bedroom, it's typically on a wooden back with stand and hanging options. Replacement rosettes can usually be found from independent online shops.

VINTAGE FLORAL
A small Barbola Mirror
from Europe 1920s-30s.
A girly romantic moment.

DRESSING MIRROR
(Also known as a cheval mirror)

A freestanding dressing mirror
is as much functional as it
contributes to the décor in a
bedroom. If wall space is scarce it's
a good solution. And the ability to
pivot and angle the mirror is an
added benefit.

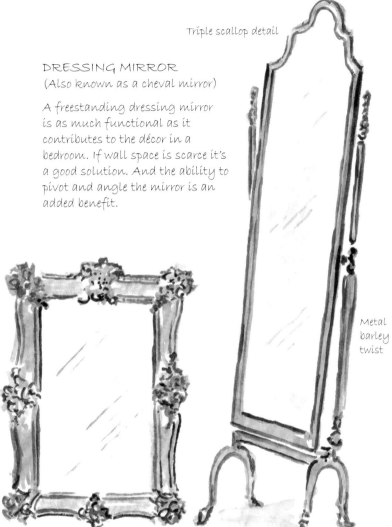

Metal
barley
twist

THE PRINCE MIRROR
A classic. Easily placed,
horizontally or vertically.
Gold finish with crumbly
white plaster peeking
through. Handsome
and elegant.

MUTED MOLDING MIRRORS
A few feet of peeling and crumbling
salvaged molding can easily
transform into a mirror. Understated,
unpretentious but still poetic.

Shabby pink

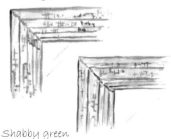

Shabby blue

Shabby green

FLORENTINE MADE IN ITALY

In their early life they may have had an air of
pretentiousness, demanding to be center of attention.
But over time their gaudy gold finish takes on a softer glow.
And now their value comes from their unassuming elegance.

I place Florentine pieces comfortably in a vintage setting,
where they blend in with other timeworn beauties, as well
as in a modern setting, as a quirky statement.

MAGAZINE RACK
Made originally for magazines, could
bring a faded glamour moment to an
office or bathroom for storage.

Bowed sides, flat front

FOREVER ELEGANT
Little dresser for anywhere.

Scallop-edged top

FLORENTINE

Authentic Florentine is made from very lightweight wood. Sometimes the legs are screwed in for easy transporting. Be mindful that there are some later plastic versions, although they are quite convincing to the eye so would still create the look. Also note: the earlier wood versions are not waterproof so pretty doilies or coasters would be in keeping with the aesthetic while protecting the paint finish.

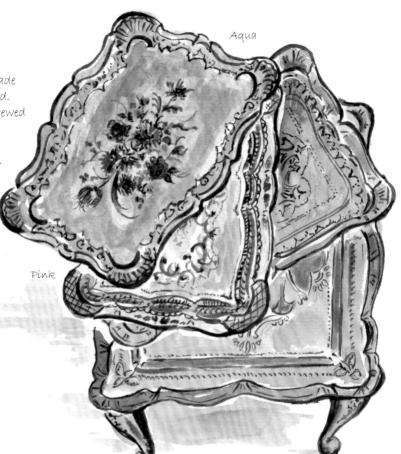

Aqua

Pink

Dainty legs

LAVISH TRAYS

While Florentine is predominantly gold, it's the accent colors that bring them to life. I, of course, love the accent colors in shades of my palette of pale blues and pinks, through to raspberry and teal, which are a little rarer than the more commonly found darker greens and reds.

BIG LITTLE DETAILS

Houses from days gone by typically have lots of big and little details
that I find interesting, charming, and worthy of being treasured.
It's sad to me when they have not been protected in someone's process
of renovation. To me that is removing little parts of the soul from
a home, as well as its beauty. Over the years of homes I have restored
(and in some instances, unrestored), I have worked out solutions
to reinstate the soul, piece by piece, bringing back those details
and restoring the dignity of the home.

Some of these details can be incorporated into homes of a more modern
or minimal aesthetic, to give subtle interesting moments where a
blank canvas can benefit from some warmth, texture, and whimsy.

"Where there is ruin, there is hope for a treasure."

Rumi

sympathetic restoration

There are many sources to explore when gathering elements for restoration.
Salvage and reclamation yards are treasure troves for salvaged columns,
molding, floorboards, and tiles. It takes a little more patience and
understanding from carpenters and builders, working out quantities
needed and installation requirements, but the process becomes a labor
of love for all involved, and there is a wonderful sense of pride in
participating in the process of restoring a home back to its days of glory.

So, I consider salvage and reclamation yards safe havens, housing these
architectural treasures, rescued after demolition, separated from the
context of their past life, and understanding their value as individuals.
And that their imperfections of peeling paint, chips, and cracks make
them unique and beautiful, adding value.

And the day will come when they find their home, in the hands of
someone who will cherish them, placing them meaningfully just where
they belong, and it will no longer matter they were once part of a bigger
story, they will radiate in their own glory. Perhaps now as a mirror or
support of a wall, but wherever they land they will no longer be considered
a "has been" but a valuable contribution to the beauty of a home.

Flaky blue paneling with medallions
and rose swages

These salvaged beauties can only have come from what must have been
a beautiful home, once upon a time.

ARCHITECTURAL WONDERS
One can't help but wonder what bigger story glamorous
architectural components were once part of. Perhaps a room of
carved rose swagged paneling from a formal 18th-century ballroom,
or Corinthian fluted columns of an entryway to a gorgeous home.
Sad to think what their home once was is no longer.

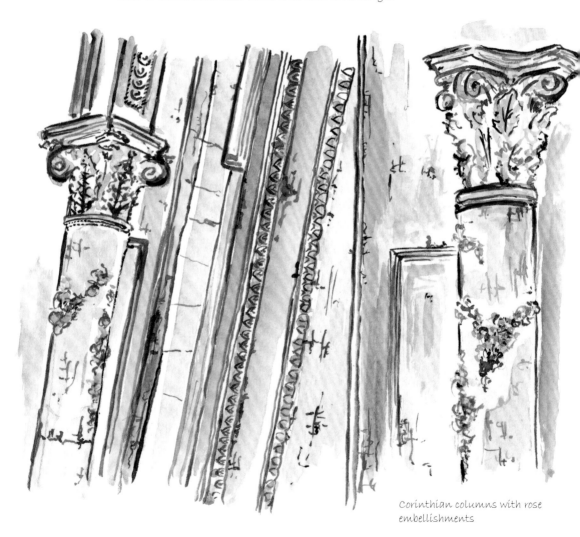

Corinthian columns with rose
embellishments

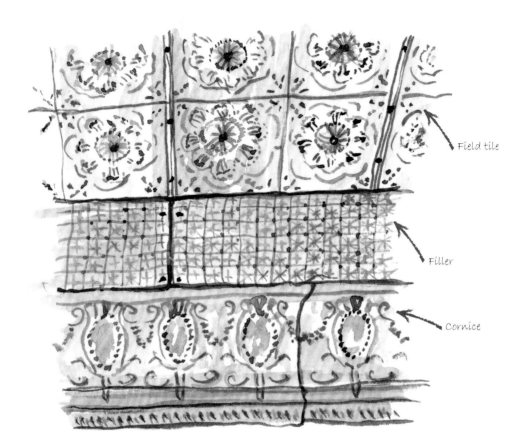

Field tile

Filler

Cornice

FANCY TIN

Tin ceilings have always been a trademark in my Shabby Chic stores. They give my twinkling chandeliers a backdrop of faded glamour and bring a timeless elegance to pair well with patinaed walls and wonky wooden floors. In the right home, tin ceilings can be an elaborate and elegant addition.

Tin ceilings were first introduced in the US in the 1800s. They were typically painted white to emulate ornate plasterwork from Europe. As well as in private homes, tin ceilings and wainscoting (wooden paneling on walls) became popular installations in commercial spaces, churches, libraries, banks, train stations, and hotels. My favorite uses of them today are in bathrooms, kitchens, and hallways (in hallways they work beautifully with Anaglypta wallpaper).

There are many companies today continuing this legacy of stamping designs on square tin tiles. They are installed by being attached to a metal framework dropped from a ceiling.

A tin ceiling is a combination of three components:

1. Field panels. Covers the entire ceiling.

2. Filler. Creates a low-profile border around the filled tiles.

3. Cornice. Transitions from ceiling to wall.

majestic corner

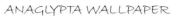

When complementary authentic details come together, they create a rich and scrumptious space, whether a whole room, a nook, or a hallway.

ANAGLYPTA WALLPAPER

Anaglypta wallpaper is one of the oldest techniques of wallpaper developed by Thomas Palmer in 1887. Anaglypta paper is an embossed paintable wallpaper. The name Anaglypta is taken from the Greek meaning "raised cameo," maybe one of the earliest embossed patterns was a cameo.

Anaglypta paper is typically installed and painted in stairways and dining rooms, from the floor up to around 3ft (90cm) to the chair or dado rail height.

My mama always had Anaglypta paper with a geometric embossed design lining the entryway, more of an affordable function than a design feature. Easily refreshed and repainted from inevitable scuffs of life.

Semi-gloss is my preferred paint finish to apply to Anaglypta paper for a subtle sheen. But in English pubs, where anaglypta paper is often used, a high-gloss finish allows for paper to be wiped down for cleaning.

Because Anaglypta paper is usually only installed halfway up walls and sparingly throughout a home, it's an opportunity to introduce a complementary palette when choosing the color to paint the paper or the wall above. Although, because of the appealing designs of the embossing, painting it plain white emphasizes the pattern subtly and beautifully.

Once separated by a dado rail, the wall above the Anaglypta can be painted or a contrasting wallpaper installed. It can also be beautiful to wallpaper a full wall or room from floor to ceiling in Anaglypta paper.

VINTAGE WALLPAPER

Vintage wallpaper is a decorative passion of mine, and I am particularly drawn to floral designs from the 1940s and '50s. The printing process back then created more texture of the painted pattern and the colors took on a saturating beauty. Often only a couple of rolls of the same design can be found, in which case you have to use sparingly. Pairing with Anaglypta paper is an attractive and authentic balance and reduces the amount of vintage paper needed. Choosing small spaces or wallpapering one wall in a room are other solutions for limited quantities.

Vintage wallpaper usually needs to have paste applied and it can be brittle, so care is needed when installing. Often the seams are a little more evident than newer paper, but this is an acceptable imperfection. A charming detail is the selvaged edge, where the manufacture and

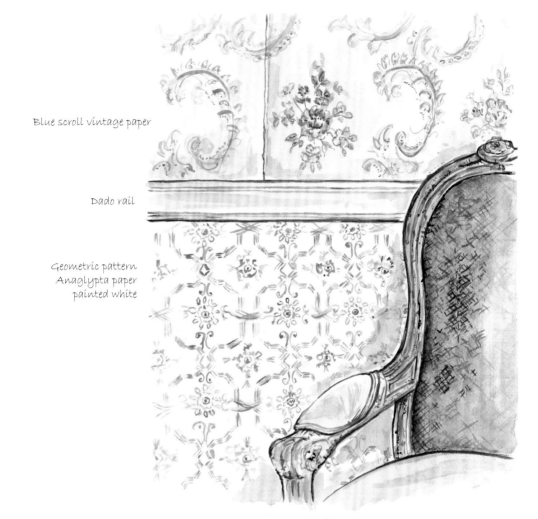

Blue scroll vintage paper

Dado rail

Geometric pattern
Anaglypta paper
painted white

color keys are placed. This also served as a protection of the ends of the rolls
of wallpaper, but for installation the selvaged edge has to be cut off or
layered over. Finding and installing vintage wallpaper is another example
of when patience is needed, but the end result is evidence of restoring a home
sympathetically to its era as well as a unique decorative statement.

DADO RAILS

Dado rails are usually installed on a wall about 3ft (90cm) from the floor.
Originally the purpose of a dado rail was to prevent backs of chairs from
damaging wall coverings in dining rooms. Be mindful if placing on a
stairway or through a hallway to choose a molding with little protrusion
so as not to encroach on the space. They should nearly always be painted
a gloss bright white. If you have other molding in your house, they should
be complementary in detail and size.

all about the details

When renovating or restoring a home, it's important to make decisions that are sympathetic and mindful to the bones and the soul of the home. Even if buying reproduction hardware, I am careful to choose pieces that have authentic qualities rather than a version with a modern twist. When choosing paint colors and finishes, I pay close attention to traditional choices from days gone by. These subtle little choices play a role in the end result feeling as though it belongs, and that it was always there with just having had a refresh.

Ornate frame for wall paneling or a mirror

CARVED EMBELLISHMENTS
For the home or a treasure.

There are multiple options to restore or embellish a home or a found treasure.

These little details can elevate something from mediocrity to gorgeousness. Some are carved wood, some made from a composition.

Sometimes a tiny touch is needed, or you could reach for the world of Versailles and use an abundance. Either way, I always research for inspiration so that I use in accordance with what looks authentic. Paint finish is also an important consideration, from glossy to chalky depending on installation.

Square medallions (perhaps for a plain or damaged piece of vintage wall or frame)

Tiny trims to add to crown molding

PLAYFUL STENCIL
Our homes are a place to reflect our personalities and be a safe place for our creative expression. The playful art form of stenciling is an opportunity to do so either on walls or floors. Options to buy custom-design stencils are limitless. A delicate Victorian floral or primitive icons can bring that unique additional layer of personality and definition of design.

Medallion cross on floor

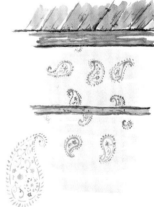

Primitive paisley on wall

THE PAINTED STAIRWAY
A painted carpet.

It's always a welcome sight to see painted stairways, sometimes glossy, sometimes well-trodden and wearing away. I have adopted this many times over. If the treads of the steps are attractive, I leave a border. From time to time they may have to be retouched or repainted, but it's a whimsical alternative to a stair runner.

Border left unpainted

High gloss painted treads

White wall above

Pale blue half wall

HALF-PAINTED WALL
I find inspiration on my travels and in movies which I log away in the decorative ideas department of my thoughts.

In Morocco, Greece, and India it is customary to paint half walls. Sometimes subtle tones, sometimes with dramatic differences (the TV show **The Durrells** offers a wealth of wall detail and palette inspiration).

I love this technique as even though I love to paint a home white as the main stage, painting half walls is a quiet or dramatic way to introduce other tones. A half wall enables the lower portion to bring warmth and color without taking away from the fresh and bright stage of white.

In this instance no additional molding is needed for separating, just some tape and a steady hand for a clean line.

It's a nice subtle touch to paint the lower color half in slightly more of a sheen than the white above.

washing basins

Bathrooms are one of the most important rooms to make a statement and set the tone of décor for the home. On occasion breathtaking vintage treasures can be found, but they can take a lot of restoration, from refinishing to removing stains to finding compatible plumbing. I think finding the balance of clean and fresh and character is important for a bathroom so typically I start with being inspired by the details from days gone by and look for authentic reproduction versions.

FLORAL BOWL
I bought this many years ago and am still looking for the perfect home for it. Beautiful cascading royal blue flowers decorate the delicate shape of the porcelain sink. While preferable to have a mixer faucet, I compromised to keep the single hot and cold faucet so the charm is intact.

PRETTY LEGS
If a bathroom doesn't need extra storage by way of a built-in vanity, I always elect for a pedestal or console style sink. In this instance exposed plumbing is part of the beauty. Polished nickel is my favorite, but chrome or polished brass are also lovely options.

SIMPLE SHUTTERS
Installing interior shutters in lieu of curtains is something to consider. Standard sizes can be purchased or custom sizes are simple for a handyman to make, and it's a nice opportunity to bring in an additional accent of color into a room.

Large porcelain doorknob

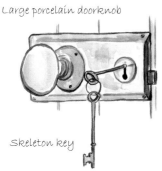
Skeleton key

LITTLE DETAILS, BIG KEY
An old-fashioned skeleton key and lock is a timeless and handsome option compatible in modern or traditional farmhouses. Often, they are a little quirky in their function, needing a jiggle, but that only adds to the charm. Newly made as attractive as vintage.

small details matter

Exquisite moments.

Doorways that we enter into and depart through are
dividers of experiences in our homes. And I believe
accents of exquisite details bring a mindfulness
to the experience of how we live in our homes,
and how we value our homes and ourselves.
Wherever we can plant beauty is an
expression of love and brings soul into
our homes.

Gathering these little treasures can be done
over time. Perhaps even before you have
anywhere to place them. They are easy to keep
safe until you know where they will bring
a bigger meaning than the seemingly small
detail that they are.

Porcelain hand-painted
finger plates (love these,
easily installed)

Rubbed brass
Victorian door set

Embossed Victorian doorknob

Porcelain knobs

chapter 4
PRETTY PALETTE

Color is an emotional form of communication without words. Shades of colors and hues evoke feelings. Pastels pertain to sensitivity and serenity, which are core values in my design work. I look to color to bring calm and harmony within my signature palette. While I am drawn to soft and faded florals and barely-there shades of vintage furniture, I like to counterbalance with whispers of the darker shades of pale to give an anchor to my otherwise wistful, romantic palette.

rainbow of colors in the shabby chic palette

blue

Sky blue, baby blue, cornflower blue, aqua, indigo, robin's egg.

Shabby Chic in nature. The sky and ocean. Linens, vintage finds, paint. Ajna, the "third eye" chakra.

MEANING
Tranquility, supports, stability, loyalty, sincerity

FEELINGS
Calm, peace, honesty, confidence

EXPRESSION
"True blue." Trustworthy and faithful

"Feeling blue." Sadness

"Out of the blue." Unexpected

brown

Taupe, chocolate, flax, bisque, mink, oatmeal.

Fabrics, furniture, wood.

MEANING
Reliable, stable, honest

FEELINGS
Grounding, stabilizes, protective

purple

Lavender, lilac, violet,

Shabby Chic faded grandeur. Royalty. Vintage china, decorative pillows. Sahasrara, the "crown" chakra.

MEANING
Nobility, luxury, grandeur, imagination

FEELINGS
Sacred, spiritual, nostalgia, dignity, healing

pink

Fuchsia, magenta, rose, blush, ballet slippers, baby pink.

Signature romantic bed linens, blush velvet, floral prints, and flowers.

MEANING
Romance, love, nurture

FEELINGS
Passion, tenderness, inner peace

EXPRESSIONS
"In the pink." Healthy

"Tickled pink." Happiness

gray

Dove, charcoal, smoky, stone.

Subdued addition in Shabby Chic for mood. Lampshades, rugs, upholstery.

MEANING
Neutral, practical

FEELINGS
Stabilizes, calms, soothes

faded orange

Rust, citrus, sunset.

Whispering accent. Shabby Chic counterbalance used sparingly. Floral prints to anchor barely-there palette. Svadhishthana, the "sacral" chakra.

MEANING
Joy, creativity

FEELINGS
Happiness, balance, stimulation

silver

Tarnished, polished, patina.

Shabby Chic glamour. Leather, vintage serving pieces, mirrors, lighting.

MEANING
Glamorous, graceful, sophisticated

FEELINGS
Elegant, positive

turquoise

Teal, aqua, blue green.

Shabby Chic signature brighter shade of pale. Vintage furniture, wallpaper, paint. Vishuddha, the "throat" chakra.

MEANING
Tranquility, serenity, prosperity, clarity

FEELINGS
Calming, emotional balance, love, joy

white

Antique, snow, pearl, ivory, chalk, whitewash.

The core of Shabby Chic. Slipcovers, detailed and simple linens, flaky vintage furniture.

MEANING
Purity, innocence, illumination, faith, beginnings

FEELINGS
Clarity, renewal, purification

EXPRESSIONS
"White as snow." Pure, clean, innocent

"White flag." Surrender

"White knight." Noble hero

green

Sage, mint, lime, sea green.

Background role in Shabby Chic. Fabric, wallpaper, chippy vintage furniture. Anahata, the "heart" chakra.

MEANING
Balance and growth

FEELINGS
Generosity, hope

yellow

Lemon, gold, mustard, mellow yellow.

Shabby Chic surprise. Velvet, apparel, flowers. Manipura, the "solar plexus" chakra.

MEANING
Clarity, optimism, enlightenment

FEELINGS
Clarifies, positivity, inspires

PALETTE & PATINA

When scanning the rows at flea markets, my eyes are drawn
to pieces of vintage in my favorite color palettes.

Shades of pink, blue, green, neutrals.

Sometimes the proportions and scale are
quite simple, sans carving. But it's all
about the patina and shades of paint.

Pinky lavender is one of my favorite shades
of pink. Not too sweet but still girly.

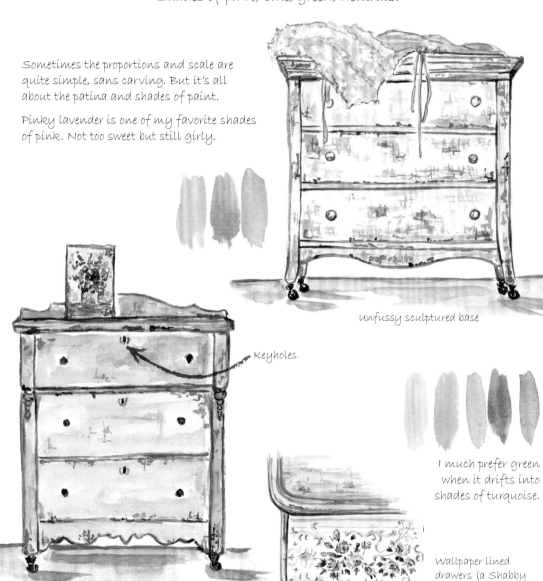

Unfussy sculptured base

Keyholes

I much prefer green
when it drifts into
shades of turquoise.

Wallpaper lined
drawers (a Shabby
Chic "restoring, ready
for loving" signature)

Caster wheels

Tiled backboard
with scallop top

IMPERFECTLY PERFECT

Beauty and function for any room in the house. Lower cabinet, drawer, top surface, back splash.

The shades of blue are reminiscent of a well-loved pair of jeans. Just the right amount of fading in all the right places.

Love, love, love...

Tarnished drawer
pulls

Worn light to
medium shade
of blue

Pretty turned-wood legs

Elegant pivot brace

QUINTESSENTIAL SHABBY CHIC

If I dreamed what my perfect piece of furniture would be, it would be this. Her beauty by way of the perfect pink layered over her prior white coat, her genteel hardware, and the elegant bowed brace supporting her lightly mottled mirror are everything I love about vintage furniture.

I'm always curious when pieces like these have keyholes, evidence that way back precious belongings were kept here.

Keyholes

Lacy tarnished
hardware

RASPBERRY DELIGHT
The combination of the authentically cracked raspberry with a raw plank surface is perfection.

Likely a taller table in a prior life, cut down for a coffee table (around 17in [43cm] tall). In its "forever-to-keep" home.

Cut down leg

PROUDLY PINK
Her chunky proportions and no-fuss demeanor are made feminine by her coat of pale pink paint.

SHADES OF PINK HARVEST TABLE

Pink represents love, innocence, and gentleness. Even on this hardworking harvest table, the pinkness gives her a femininity.

I love harvest tables, knowing that their purpose of place is for gathering the fruits of labor. They are usually 6ft (1.8m) long (or more), made from joined planks. And the legs are typically hinged for easy storing. They are often painted in my favorite palette of pale pinks and pale greens, weathered and sun bleached from being outside.

Planks

Hinged folding legs

TEN SHADES OF GREEN

I don't always love green but I do when it's faded and worn. I also love that it is the color of anahata, the fourth "heart" chakra.

Turned wood legs

WATERCOLOR FOR THE SOUL
KIM MCCARTY

Kim and I have been friends for 20 years, so I have had a front row seat observing the many chapters of her journey and evolution as an artist. Kim's subject and palette move me. Soft and calming with highlights of intrigue. The ethereal qualities in her work captivate my mind and engage my eyes with the depth and detail of her use of color.

Watercolor is her chosen medium which she explains is a fluid process, where she applies watercolor to moist paper, never certain how the colors will fall, often having to try many attempts to create her vision. Visiting her studio in Malibu, CA is breathtaking, her ethereal space is the perfect stage for her poignant work.

Like blurry afterimages drifting past closed eyelids,
Kim McCarty's watercolors hover between presence and absence,
innocence and wisdom, and past, present, and future. Working
rapidly at times using only a single color and at other times
a haunting, bruise-inspired palette of acid yellows,
greens, and browns.

BOHO BEAUTY

"Blessed is the influence of one true, loving human soul on another."
George Eliot

SUNSHINE

"I think of love, and you, and my heart grows full and warm, and my breath stands still... I can feel sunshine stealing into my soul and making it all summer, and every thorn a rose."

Emily Dickinson

INNOCENCE

Don't forget to remember me.

GOODBYE GIRL

"Goodbyes are only for those who love with their eyes. Because for those who love with heart and soul there is no such thing as separation."

Rumi

TRUE LOVE

"Whoever lives true life, will love true love."
Elizabeth Barrett Browning

LOVERS

"Love shall be our token; love be yours and love be mine."
Christina Rossetti

FLEETING PETALS

"That it will never come again is what makes life so sweet."
Emily Dickinson

PERFECTION

"A flower blossoms for its own joy."
Oscar Wilde

PURPLE TIPS

"Our scars make us know that our past was for real."
Jane Austen

chapter 5
FABRICS GALORE

Fabrics play the role of influencing the overall ambiance in a room. Transforming bare landscapes into rich woven tapestries of texture, hue, and pattern. As sung so beautifully by Carole King in her song "Tapestry."

Fabric dresses important characters in our homes including sofas, chairs, cushions, bedding, curtains, and tables. Draped or puddling, tailored, or loose and flowing, fabric sets the tone and attitude. I always welcome signs of a life lived and loved shown in sun-bleached florals or labor-of-love applied patches enhancing the character.

Fabric choices and dressings for our homes are a reflection of our personality and can be as playful as the clothes we wear. They bring diversity from room to room. Some rooms we may gravitate to for light, while others we go to for seclusion. How we decorate with fabrics helps create the balance and value of both.

Decadent dupioni silk curtains reminiscent of a fancy ballroom can live in the same home as curtains made from a soulful linen. A serene white mushy sofa can share space with a rich vintage floral chintz chair. Harmony happens when beauty collides.

CHINTZ CHAIR

This chair with her chintzy slipcover is pure perfection to me. I came across her on a buying trip in England. For reasons I will never understand, I left her behind and didn't buy her. Maybe at the time I didn't think she was so special. But I never forgot her. And years later I went back to try and find her, but both she and the store were nowhere to be found. She lives on through the inspiration she gave me as a print, as a color palette, and as a frame for my Wallace chair. But I still look at photos I took of her and wonder why I didn't bring her home when I had the chance.

I love vintage chintz fabric. This one has a waxy glaze which is typical on English floral patterns. She has a way of evoking passion as she comes in and out of fashion. Loved during the Victorian times in England as well as in Jackie Kennedy's days at The White House, and years later loved by Princess Diana. For me she is the epitome of loveliness.

When choosing fabrics, I prioritize touch and loving how it looks and behaves rather than letting a thread count or fabric construction deemed superior be my deciding factor. That is another beauty of vintage. There is an acceptance of simply loving something for what it is, often without a label influencing our authentic judgment. I like crisp cotton sheets, drapey velvet, and crumpled damasks.

Fabrics give us the flexibility to evolve with our moods and seasons. Slipcovers can be changed out. Table linens worthy of royalty or a quiet and plain ensemble both equally have their time and place. A bedroom can take on a whole different character by the redressing of a bed. Depending on our mood we can sleep amongst a bed of flowers and frills or soothing simple white cotton sheets without having to consider changing out any furniture.

As with all decisions when decorating a home, start with being aware and seeking inspiration from movies, magazines, or places you visit. Look below the surface for details that seem magical, whether it's a piece of carefully inserted lace, how a curtain hangs, or how color makes you feel, and little by little incorporate those details into creating your own tapestry of life in your home. Trust your instincts with your choices and in doing so your home will be an authentic sanctuary.

CLASSIC SQUISHY WHITE DENIM SLIPCOVER
The most loved and easily placed sofa.

SLIPCOVERS

Slipcovered furniture is the heart of Shabby Chic. I don't take credit for creating them, but in 1989 when I began my business, the most commonly found slipcovers were made of clear plastic for the purpose of protecting furniture. Way back then I was a young mother with many years ahead of me of children with sticky fingers, so I began the not so easy task of finding an upholsterer to make me a slipcover. What began as a personal agenda of creating a home of beauty, function, and comfort for myself later spawned a movement and the introduction of perceiving slipovers in a new way, shabby and chic.

I had a specific vision of a sofa and slipcover with the function of beauty and washability. Creating the perfect sofa with mushy cushions, while dressed in a relaxed slipcover that could be washed. Like blue jeans, slipcovers become cozier and more individual with each wash and allow for furniture to be lived in, capturing memories along the way.

In my early days I curated a collection of fabrics from white denim to chenille, velvet, and floral linen. Through trial and error of learning about shrinkage and over fading, my Shabby Chic library of fabrics was born.

Some slipcovers are designed to be relaxed while others have a more tailored appeal. Either way, the ease of removing for cleaning is now an expected offering in the furnishing industry.

PURPLE PORTOBELLO
Velvet tailored slipcover. No skirt—to reveal the pretty turned wood leg with caster wheels.

Gathered arms to accommodate waterfall arms

Piping

No skirt

slipcover details

The fit and details of a slipcover are equally as important as fabric choice.

1. The upholstery underneath the slipcover is something to consider. Preferably a pale fabric so it doesn't show through the slipcover.

2. If you want a more streamlined and tailored slipcover, consider dry cleaning rather than washing. This will maintain a more contemporary and sleek aesthetic while still having the function of removing the cover rather than upholstery.

3. Details, like piping or ruffles, can be made in the same fabric as the body of the slipcover or in a contrasting fabric.

4. When choosing a fabric, be sure it has been pre-shrunk to allow for future washings. Depending on the fabric this can range from 5% to 10% shrinkage.

5. Be mindful if you choose a fabric with centered pattern (like a large floral bouquet versus floating flowers), extra yardage is needed to accommodate unusable yardage. However, wastage fabrics could be used to make accompanying decorative pillows or arm caps.

6. Make sure seams are overlocked to prevent fraying in the wash.

7. Wash at a cool temperature and take out of dryer before completely dry. It is normal when redressing the sofa for the slipcover to feel snug, but just like a pair of jeans, the fabric will soon give and reshape itself.

8. The beauty of a slipcover is if life lived leaves a mark, you can wash just that piece. Or make a pretty patch if needs be.

9. Arm caps are additional protection and a lovely layer.

10. I like zipper closures (more than Velcro), preferably use ones that blend into the color of the fabric. Always close the zippers when washing.

11. If a skirt is desired, I like the added touch of lining (make sure lining fabric has also been pre-shrunk).

12. I tend to gravitate to a relaxed slipcover, always wanting extra fabric to tuck into the back and sides of the base, and under the cushions of the sofa or chair.

13. I raised my children with sticky fingers, sand from the beach, and messy pets alongside white denim slipcovers. A splash of bleach in the wash was my savior.

Arm caps (for extra protection with ease to wash)

Full gathered ruffle

Often the washing of fabric gives it a character that I love in creating puckers and flops and even fades. In my early days of compiling my library of Shabby Chic fabrics, I was advised by others that the fabrics I had bought were not constructed for washing, for the very same reasons I believe washing transforms them with added beauty.

WING CHAIR SLIPCOVER

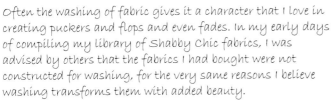

Arm caps

Flange detail

Exposed legs

SIZES OF PRE-SHRUNK MATERIAL NEEDED FOR SLIPCOVERS

Depending on size of furniture and if fabric pattern needs to be centered.

CHAIR: 9-13 yards (8.2-11.9m)
SETTEE: 17-20 yards (15.5-18.3m)
SOFA: 19-24 yards (17.4-21.9m)

Fitted boxed back cushions
(another option could be loose
backed cushions)

Piping around arms and cushions

Full ruffle joined at base
by tiny ruffle detail

Box pleat

There are a variety of trim details to
enhance the styling. Consider some will
consume more fabric than others.

Slightly gathered ruffle (my
personal favorite ruffle)

Side kick pleat

MY LOVE OF FLORAL FABRIC

Designing floral prints is a never-ending love of mine.
I am always inspired by vintage scraps and panels I find on my
travels, and often alter the colors and scale of the flowers to suit
my vision. I design mindfully so that the florals can mismatch
and layer together. Some are sweeter and little girl-like, some have
a more timeworn vintage feel, sometimes more boho and eclectic.
But the common thread of all is my attention to every little leaf
and petal, along with every placement of color, until the palette
and pattern work in harmony.

THE BEAN
Named after her frame, she can be front and center or petite enough to tuck away into a corner. She also could also live easily in a boudoir.

Her feminine demeanor looks so sweet dressed in flowers, but she still looks lovely in plain white linen or plush blush velvet. By way of her slipcover, she is a chameleon.

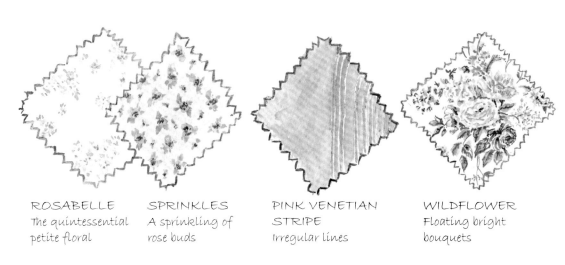

ROSABELLE
The quintessential petite floral

SPRINKLES
A sprinkling of rose buds

PINK VENETIAN STRIPE
Irregular lines

WILDFLOWER
Floating bright bouquets

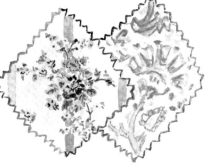
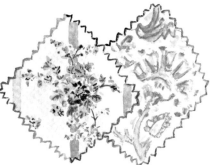
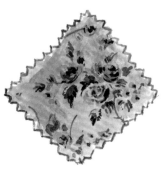

ANASTASIA
Mottled and faded blue with pink ditsy flowers

MEADOW STRIPE
Tiny bouquets nestled in a small pink stripe

INDIES
Faded blue Indian-inspired block print

OVERDYED SOMERSET
Brighter red roses overdyed with purply blue

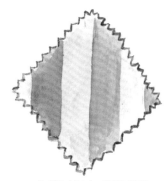

CHELSEA
Teal stage scattered with flowers and leaves

DANCING DAHLIAS
Raspberry stage with dahlias in ten different shades of pink

CABANA STRIPE
Faded blue stripe

LADIES & GENTLEMEN

The theme of mixing and matching
chairs continues over to mixing and
matching slipcovers. Along with serving
a meaningful function by way of being
machine washable, the slipcovers add a design
interest and a welcoming invitation.

MISMATCHED TRIO

The common thread of beauty is evident with this
trio. By way of the details of the slipcovers, they
all make their own unique statement in style and
details, revealing tapered oak legs, a kick-pleat
skirt to the ground, and some ruffles.

PRETTY
RENE

Floral linen slip
with short skirt

NOAH

LIBERTY

White linen short
loose ruffle skirt

White slipcover
long kick pleat

FIRST LOVE, NOAH

I love him. He was inspired by a timeworn set of six French chairs that have lived with me for many years.

I was drawn to calling my reproduced version a gentleman's name in homage to the romantic literary character Noah Calhoun from **The Notebook**. I wanted this chair to have neverending love. Noah speaks of that first love, that never goes away, and that sentiment applies to this chair for me. Many other chairs have passed through my hands, but there will never be another Noah.

A genteel chair, with graceful but sturdy legs. His back is just slightly bowed for grace and comfort, and inserted with delicate woven canework. On the tip of his back he is gently carved, beautiful without being overly fussy. Coated in the perfect shade of shabby white, rubbed down with gentle distress.

While I wanted to keep the timeworn rattan back exposed, adding a faded floral linen seat slipcover is an opportunity to add individual personality and a touch of my own personal taste. Noah would also look handsome in a plain white linen seat slipcover.

Loose ruffle

Tiny piping

Floppy linen ties

Faded floral linen chair slip

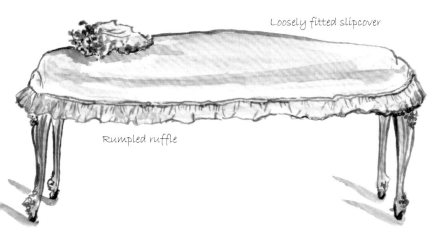

Loosely fitted slipcover

Rumpled ruffle

NOAH BENCH

Noah has a busy life due to flexibility of placement, but lives perfectly at the foot of a dreamy bed. He has fine sturdy legs, which paired with a loosely fitted slipcover detailed with a small irregular ruffle make this otherwise ordinary bench dreamy.

TUFTED TREASURES

It has been written that the Earl of Chesterfield commissioned the first Chesterfield sofa in the 1700s, with the thought that the intricate deep buttoning detail and a low seat, upholstered in quality leather, would help gentlemen to sit upright and not wrinkle their clothing. My personal favorite tufting is diamond tufting, which creates a pattern of diamonds secured with a fabric-covered button. One of the benefits of tufted furniture is that it remains plush and plumped without the need to fluff due to the tufting technique which adds extra cushioning to the raised pockets.

Tufted furniture is as wonderfully comfortable as it is beautiful. Classic diamond tufting design is romantic and cozy and a wonderful addition to the repertoire of other chosen pieces in the home.

Velvet is often the fabric of choice due to its plush feel, and is always a nice option for vintage found pieces that need reupholstering. The classic legacy lends itself to being transformed into whimsy with a playful choice of fabric.

ELEGANT WHIMSY

I have forever loved this four-seater round diamond-tufted beauty placed at the entryway of the country hotel, Babington House in Somerset. Her hot pink fabric dressing brings a sense of informality to her otherwise intimidating form.

TUFTED OTTOMAN
Traditional by nature, made inviting with comfy tufts.

Diverse in use, it could sit next to a coffee table with an accompanying tray as well as at the end of a bed.

PRINCESS SETTEE
Her tufted back steals the show, combined with a simple upholstered seat.

PILLOWS & CUSHIONS

While they are considered an accent, decorative pillows are the finishing touch that adds the layer of completion. They can bring a unique personality into a home and be a perfect invitation to a sofa or chair. They may be a small accessory, but they can be exactly what makes that "je ne sais quoi" mystery moment, where everything just ties together. It is important to gather with patience, because it's how they harmonize together that brings the magic. And it takes time to cast all the players.

FLOP & MUSH

I love an array of fabrics—velvet, vintage leftovers, linen florals. But the most important to me is the right amount of "flop" and "mush." With the right amount of fill and the right fabric, if a pillow could talk it would say "you are welcome here." I am not a fan of pillows perfectly lined up with a karate chop, for they feel intimidating in their uniformed perfection.

So, give choice of pillows the time and thought it deserves to help nurture their contribution to the harmony of a room.

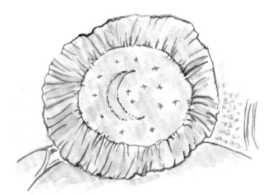

While looking for the moon we found some stars along the way.

Velvet

Silk

Floral

AN ARMFUL OF PILLOWS
An eclectic mix of round mushy pillows gathered around a central panel.

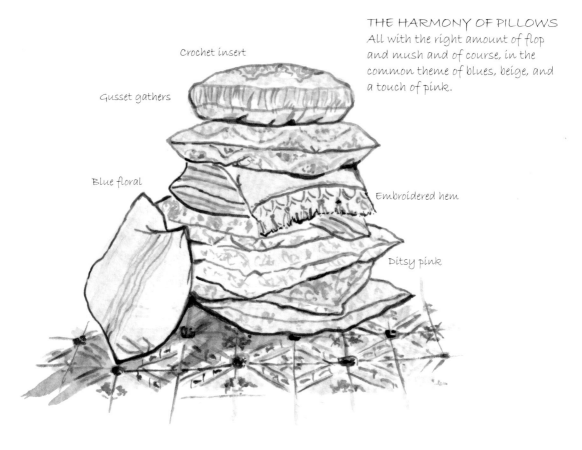

THE HARMONY OF PILLOWS
All with the right amount of flop and mush and of course, in the common theme of blues, beige, and a touch of pink.

Crochet insert

Gusset gathers

Blue floral

Embroidered hem

Ditsy pink

LOVE embroidery

Gathered ruched edge

Ditsy pink roses

I LOVE YOU PILLOW
While silent pillows say so much, an embroidered message is a welcomed personal touch.

LABOR OF LOVE NEEDLEPOINT

Needlepoint pillows are the crème de la crème when bringing a depth of beauty, uniqueness, and meaningful details as part of an ensemble of decorative pillows.

I rarely pass up needlepoint pillows when I find them, especially if sewn in my palette and in a classic floral design. As a collection they are divine or, when singularly added in with pillows of other fabrications, they are a treasured handmade accent. They come with history and emotion, knowing they were once upon a time someone's labor of love, made with patience and pride for creating something beautiful. At times I find completed works, not yet made into something. In those cases, I sew them into pillows, sometimes adding a velvet border detail. And then sometimes I find nearly complete pieces, revealing the stencil or hand drawing of what was left unfinished. But even those, I will make into a pillow as they were found, as a statement that "the unfinished beauty is beauty enough."

SYMPHONY OF ROSES STITCHED ONE BY ONE

Velvet panel

Wool fringe detail

RUFFLES & FLANGES

Choice of details on a
pillow can be a feminine
voice or just a simple
statement.

Thin welt

2½in (6.4cm)
straight flange

THIN WELT

2½" FLANGE

Shirred
(gathered) welt

Floppy
ruffle

Full FLOPPY RUFFLE

SHIRRED WELT

Double ruffle

double RUFFLE

Standard raw
edge ruffle

Tiny flange

standard ruffle

TINY FLANGE

Two-sided petite
corner ruffle

2 SIDED CORNER RUFFLE

Grand majesty

Rose blossom

ROSE MAJESTY

A "forever-to-keep" Shabby Chic print.

Quintessentially oversized cabbage roses
with shaded sage leaves.

SHABBY STRONG

As a designer sometimes my focus is simply to design the loveliest of things I can. But at other times there is a story to be told.

As I designed this pillow, I had a story to tell, I wanted to incorporate different emotions.

I chose the palette for its gentility.
I chose the linen for its softness.
I chose the embroidery for strength.
I chose the embroidered birds for freedom.

WINDOW DRESSING

There is something rather grown up and proper about traditional curtains. And with all the available bells and whistles of details and variety of linings possible, along with the amount of fabric needed they are a considered expense.

Until later in my life I was a lace panel, thumb tack girl. Not only for the affordability and the romantic aesthetic but also, I love the impermanence and non-attachment, especially in my days of renting homes. The lyrics in Dido's song, "Life for Rent," have always resonated with me on this subject.

Over time as I have settled, I have committed to proper curtains (albeit sparingly), especially where I want privacy or desire to sleep past dawn.

Window dressing is a commitment to a point of view of decorating a room, by way of print, color, and the choice of details of the headers, from ruching to rod pockets.

I welcome the visible effects of sun bleaching on a bolder floral print, adding a layer of imperfection, the balance of shabby and chic.

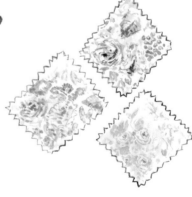

COUNTRY CURTAINS
There is a time for a bold statement. My preference is for them to soften by fading and have gentle gathers sewn into rings to naturally cause imperfection and diffuse fussiness.

ROMAN BOHO
A French flavor adds an accent of boho.

The relaxed Roman shade is an option
for a smaller window where a pair of
curtains might seem too cumbersome.

Ruched ties
for raising
and lowering

Sweet ruffle

PRETTY LITTLE SHADE
She sits within a formal setting of a
traditional frame, giving some whimsy
(installed with tension rod).

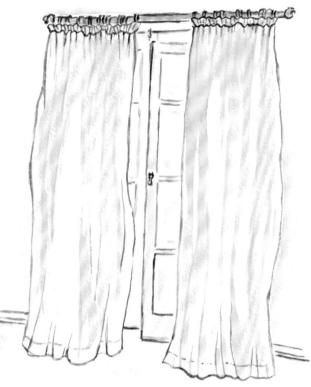

BLUSH SILK DUPIONI

These have graced my windows in my bedroom for years. Handmade with great skill of hand-smocking and ruffled header.

The rings are sewn in, so the hand smocking isn't disturbed by hooks, which was a process to remove and sew back in when I had the curtains cleaned.

I opted for a blackout liner (with a heavier white liner to obscure the blackout).

Good quality blackouts serve in both keeping light at bay as well as muffling sound, giving a feeling of stillness and silence.

Each evening it is a ritual for me to mindfully close them and give a pause for the day behind me. And each morning as I let in the light, I give gratitude to the day ahead.

The movement of the wooden rings on the wooden pole is a soothing sound.

Wooden pole, bracket, and rings

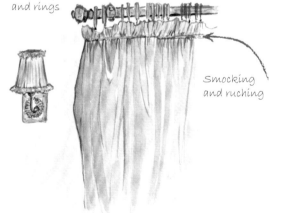

Smocking and ruching

TINY BANNER

While letting in the light, this is effective for privacy, perhaps in a bathroom.

LACE & THUMBTACKS
My signature window covering when privacy is not an issue.

Typically vintage found, romantic, and breezy.

SIMPLE FANCY
An otherwise simple white linen panel is caped with a vintage found floral valance.

Hung at ceiling level to give as much height as possible.

HEADBOARDS

A place for our heads to rest. Deciding on the fabric for our beds is an important choice to the overall aesthetic of our beds and bedroom. While headboards have their own character, they need to have the ability to complement the choice of dressings of bed linens.

SLIPCOVERED HEADBOARD
The most practical of all for ease of washing and changing out slipcover as desired.

Aqua rose floral

Pale blue velvet

TUFTING FOR DREAMS
Comfy and elegant as well as timeless.

ANTIQUE FRENCH BED

Due to its muted woven silk jacquard upholstery,
I consider this a neutral beauty. As stunning as she
is, she falls into the background, never to overwhelm.

BEDDING BEAUTIES

While our bedroom is our sanctuary, our bedding is the fabric with which we layer our nests. It's where we should seek perfection in feeling comforted and safe. Our bed linen is like a cloak of nurture for our soul.

The choice of bedding is vast and personal. I prefer crisp poplin cotton over silky sateen or breezy linen so give yourself the honor to consider and make the choice of what is right for you.

The dressing of our bed takes us through the first thoughts as we wake, our final thoughts of the day, and our time to dream. Whether frills and ruffles, flowers and lace, or simple white linens, our lives are positively affected by being mindful of how we dress this sacred space.

PARADISE FLORAL
Teals and purple scattered florals layered with flax linen, sans frills or ruffles.

Dressing for our dreams.

PINK EMBROIDERED HEM

Overly generous hem makes
her presence known

CLUNY
Inspired by vintage
trim on tablecloth.

Scallop-edged bed ruffle

DOUBLE RUFFLE
Abundant.

LINEN TRIMS & TREATS

I'm as passionate about designing trims and details
for bedding collections as I am about designing prints.

The legacy of my mum's collection of vintage scraps of
trims lives on through my work. As a child I was
bemused by the value she bestowed on the teeniest
tiniest scraps that may have held a precious little
detail, now I seek inspiration for my work from the
hidden and overlooked tiny saved leftovers, that then
become the heart of something beautiful.

Along with my classical floral collection, white is
signature to my bedding design work, and is often
where these delicate details find their voice. As always,
I love to see all the little details combined to make for
a hodgepodge of white wonder.

CAPRI
All white except for tiny
cotton trim with bows.

Cotton underskirt

Lace ruffle

LACE DUST RUFFLE
Originally I would tuck a lace curtain under my mattress as a pretend dust ruffle, until I designed one. I purposefully wanted the fine lace to puddle abundantly for an extra opportunity to be noticed.

MONOGRAM
I buy monogramed linens at the brocante markets in France regardless of the initials of the monogram. But when the opportunity presents itself to monogram treasures, it's a personal touch like no other. The font of choice can complement the fabric, whether for an English manor or a country cottage, along with the choice of thread being a bold shade or quietly white. It's a special addition of meaning and value.

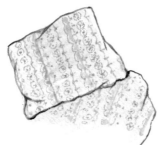

PINK BOHO
Embroidery with a boho flair.

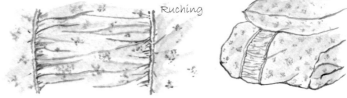

Ruching

DITSY RUCHED
In lieu of a lace detail, I chose a gathered ruched insert for a subtle but pretty little detail, a signature in many of my bed linen designs.

lovely lace

Lace is an important element in my design work. It allows me to subtly or abundantly bring whimsy and special little details into a plain and simple stage.

Sometimes a teeny tiny insert is all that is needed and sometimes an abundance of puddling lace speaks volumes on romance.

My mum always gave me a piece of linen and lace come gift giving time. Sometimes a tablecloth, sometimes a pillow sham. My collection has been a wealth of inspiration in my designing as well as giving me years of enjoyment from these handmade, one of a kind precious presents. I have never seen or received a vintage piece that isn't truly beautiful.

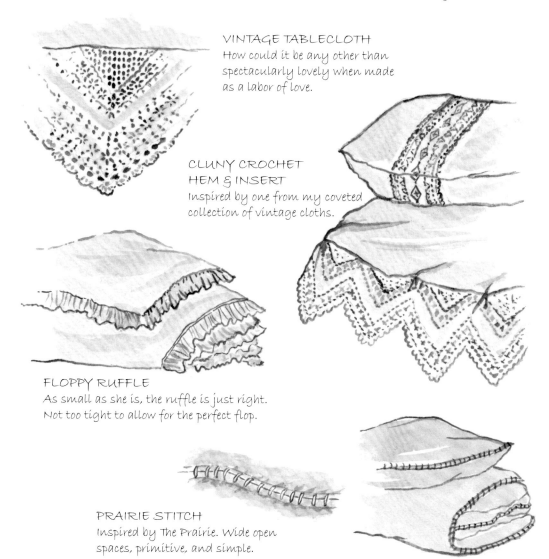

VINTAGE TABLECLOTH
How could it be any other than spectacularly lovely when made as a labor of love.

CLUNY CROCHET
HEM & INSERT
Inspired by one from my coveted collection of vintage cloths.

FLOPPY RUFFLE
As small as she is, the ruffle is just right. Not too tight to allow for the perfect flop.

PRAIRIE STITCH
Inspired by The Prairie. Wide open spaces, primitive, and simple.

THE LINEN CUPBOARD

One of the most important and pleasing cupboards in our homes. It's where we house the fabrics on which we dream.

Therefore, I prioritize a place to keep these treasures. Whether a built-in cabinet or freestanding cupboard, I make the effort to wallpaper the backs, sides and shelves, preferably with vintage wallpaper because the process of printing from days gone by allows for depth of color and texture rarely found today. My reasoning is where we hold our linens is a sacred space, and it should be decorated as such, so we when we view our picks of bedding it is an experience.

If the space allows, labeling shelves with sizes is both a nice sight to see as well as creating order.

I get great joy from opening my cupboard, and seeing ruffles and ruching, sharing space with clean white linens, beautifully and orderly. Don't overstack, let go of what you don't need, so what has value can breathe and be seen.

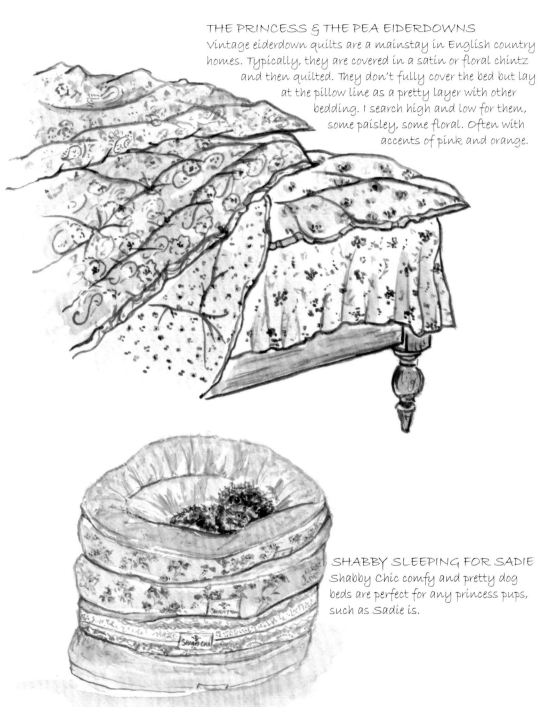

THE PRINCESS & THE PEA EIDERDOWNS
Vintage eiderdown quilts are a mainstay in English country homes. Typically, they are covered in a satin or floral chintz and then quilted. They don't fully cover the bed but lay at the pillow line as a pretty layer with other bedding. I search high and low for them, some paisley, some floral. Often with accents of pink and orange.

SHABBY SLEEPING FOR SADIE
Shabby Chic comfy and pretty dog beds are perfect for any princess pups, such as Sadie is.

PETTICOAT DRESSING

I find endless inspiration for details in fashion and theater. This tablecloth was made from pale blue linen, ruffled like a skirt with her layered lace under-petticoat, elements inspired from a costume at an opera I had seen. Layers and layers of ruffles joined by a little ruffled trim gives a flop and flounce not usually found in a tablecloth. I later did an eyelet version for a restaurant I designed for Jennifer Lopez, reminding her of a stage costume she had once worn. The beauty of looking at fashion for inspiration is that there are often intricate details not typically translated into products for the home.

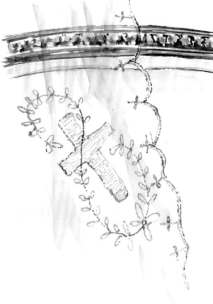

DAINTY LACE CROSS

INCOMPLETE PINK STITCHES

From time to time I come across projects that were never
completed. A rose painting with pencil lines never painted.
Or a tapestry left midway through the story. I have
treasured this embroidery for many years, wondering why?
What stopped the completion? Was it boredom, tragedy, or
the acceptance that there is beauty in the incompleteness.

chapter 6
DRESS UP AND MAKE BELIEVE

I have warm and nostalgic childhood memories from observing the hustle and bustle in creating worlds of make believe, behind the scenes of school plays. Peeking behind the curtains in wonderment, as fantasy came to life while the sets and costumes were being made. This was the most exciting part of the process for me, much more so than being in the play itself.

I felt all cozy inside seeing parents sewing and painting, one stitch or brush stroke at a time, creating the costumes and setting the stage for the storytelling to take place.

When I became a parent, I also found great joy amongst my hectic life, to be back behind the scenes when creative hands were needed to help bring the stories to life.

In my design work I have always gravitated toward hauntingly beautiful vintage costumes. They bring a theatrical quality into my story telling. Mostly ballet tutus and pointe shoes, Pierrot costumes, and endless headpieces, from floppy vintage hats to tiaras. They are always made by hand, I'm sure with the same labor of love that I observed as a little girl, and sometimes misshapen by alterations as they change performers. Seeing what in its heyday was the belle of the ball evolve overtime with grace, albeit with some tattered edges. The many stages these costumes have performed upon give these precious pieces a colorful history with unique souls.

THE ROYAL OPERA HOUSE
The most glorious theater in Covent Garden, UK. Founded in 1946, it houses the
Royal Opera, the Royal Ballet, and the Royal Orchestra. It is the third theater built
on this site, the two built prior burnt down in fires in the 1800s.

TUTUS & TULLES

Tutus are the whimsical and majestic complement to the wonderful world of ballet, supporting a ballerina to dance freely, revealing her form while decorating her every move. The ethereal quality of tulle is a fabric that whispers its presence, making a statement as though through a dream.

THE ROMANTIC TUTU
A labor of love, often taking up to 25 yards (23m) of tulle to create the multi layers of frills and ruffles. The jeweled bodices are magnificent and intricate. Each tutu has its own history, with clues about its performances and relationships with ballerinas' forms buried in its seams.

SUGAR PLUM FAIRY
Childhood dreams of being
a prima ballerina and cast
as the Sugar Plum Fairy
from **The Nutcracker**, making
Christmas all the more magical.
The dream of many little girls.

CASCADING SATIN SLIPPERS
Pointe shoes.

As beautiful as they are, and often
handmade, typically pointe shoes
only last for 20-30 hours of dancing.
Sometimes a professional ballerina
may wear one pair out in a single
performance.

Shank. The inside of the
pointe shoe, which gives
support to the arch of the foot
and hardens the sole from
the inside. The flexibility
of the shank is determined
by its thickness. Over time
it weakens and becomes
too soft and loses support.

Box. Supports and encases the
dancers' toes and allows her to
balance. Made from layers of
fabric and paper. Over time it
becomes soft and loses support.

Sole. Made of smooth
leather but can be
scratched for traction.

Fabric. Typically
a light pink satin.
Easily worn out but
once past the time of
show worthiness, often
used for rehearsal.

Two ribbons and an
elastic band, to secure
the shoes to the foot.
They are placed and sewn
in, customized to the
dancer's foot, and often
by the dancer herself.
Ribbons are wrapped
around the ankle, tied
in a double knot and
then the knot and loose
ends are tucked in
under the ribbon.

Just because something isn't real, doesn't mean it isn't beautiful. In fact, the fantasy of something lasts forever.

TWIRLING TALLULAH

I always have tutus in my home. They inspire my creative thinking with their radiance and beauty. Tallulah stops me in my tracks, slowing me down, to pause and reconnect me to my imagination.

PRETTY WHIMSY FOR PENNIES

When I create several decorative displays, I make a trip to a craft store for purposes of budget and availability of finding multiples of items. My process of letting my eyes edit, curate, and hone in on special little things is the same as when gathering treasures at the flea markets. I have trained my mind not to judge tiny details that seem like they have no value as they are jumbled within the mass, but to imagine them outside of the context and to see them as part of an elevated story. Piles of little plastic ballerinas appear on first sight to have little value, until chosen and combined with other seemingly not so special elements, and together they all rise to the occasion, with grace and pride. They just had to be found, seen, chosen, and appreciated.

Toy ballerina

Pin cushion

Posy

Ruffled doilies

MY SECRET IMAGINARY LIFE
I have always so admired ballerinas. Not just for their passion and complete dedication to their art. But for their grace and ability to freely express their heart through dance, delicately and bravely.

BELLA DONNA

My mama always had bags and boxes of "bits and bobs." She would treasure every last scrap as though they were gold and diamonds. Usually castoffs and leftovers of velvet ribbons, floppy silk scraps, and broken jewelry, they had little value on their own but once she chose them to be part of her artful creations they came into their own existence.

My mama's legacy of finding value in castoffs lives on with me. I have my own bags of "bits and bobs," the contents poised and ready to be picked for their next story in life, whether as part of meaningful gift wrappings or creating decorative table centerpieces. I have an abundance of tiny little details that bring magical layers of intrigue and beauty at my fingertips.

The perfect fitting ballet slipper contributes to a ballerina dancing with grace. But like a butterfly, a ballet slipper's life is short due to the extreme pressure on the fragile shoe.

However, their beauty continues long after their aura of dances danced, and they become wonderful decorative moments.

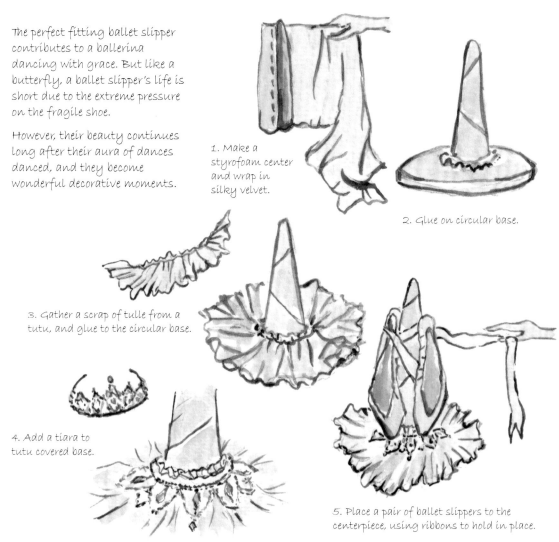

1. Make a styrofoam center and wrap in silky velvet.

2. Glue on circular base.

3. Gather a scrap of tulle from a tutu, and glue to the circular base.

4. Add a tiara to tutu covered base.

5. Place a pair of ballet slippers to the centerpiece, using ribbons to hold in place.

DANCING ON THE TABLE

THE THREE SISTERS

I never went to a prom, it wasn't an English tradition. But every prom dress that has passed through my hands causes me to pause and wonder about the dances danced in these magical dresses. I gravitate to ones made by hand with love, perhaps by a mother for her daughter's first date. The colors, the tulle, the flowers, and ruffles have a gentle innocence which accompanies the young girl as she enters her next chapter in life. While often the fabrics may not be the finest, the vision of a prom dress to me is priceless and perfect.

MY GIRLS
They will go to the ball.

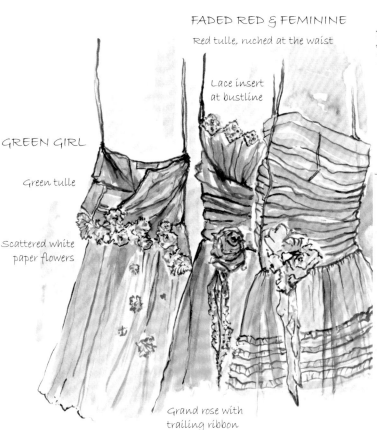

FADED RED & FEMININE
Red tulle, ruched at the waist

Lace insert at bustline

GREEN GIRL

Green tulle

Scattered white paper flowers

TEA-STAINED TULLE

Tea-stained pleated tulle

Turquoise pleated panel

Gray grand silk rose with trailing ribbon

Tea-stained tulle ruffles

Grand rose with trailing ribbon

INNOCENT BEAUTY
"Restoring for reloving" process:

Replace zippers or hooks.
If the waist or bodice is too small, insert an elastic panel on the sides.

Dye to suit color preference.
Add a ribbon sash and flowers.
Trim length for preference.

CROWNING GLORY

When completing a story of dress up and make believe, it's those little accoutrements and accents that bring the symphony together to a perfect crescendo.

Velvet petals

Crepe paper flowers

Silk blooms

Floral crown

FLORAL MANNEQUIN
A mellow silver cardboard mannequin with floppy flowers and floral crowns pinned upon it serves as an art piece in my home. Forever flowers are placed in a similar way to brush strokes on a painting. I have always loved faux flowers, for their permanence, even though they fade and flop, they last forever.

ENCHANTING
I have been a collector of vintage hats for many years. I love the delicacy of the details, tulle, floppy and teeny flowers, ribbons, and lace. Some haute couture in their early years. A captivating accessory that adds attitude, whimsy, glamour, and sophistication by their mere presence.

I've worn them with jeans and a white t-shirt for a twist of fashion as well for a finishing touch to a fancy frock.

VIOLET

TOUCH OF LUXURY

POWDER BLUE

LUSH BLOOMS

TULLE CROWN

PASTEL RAINBOW

WHIMSY
Not quite Harlequin, nor Court Jester or Clown. She's elusive in her own identity.

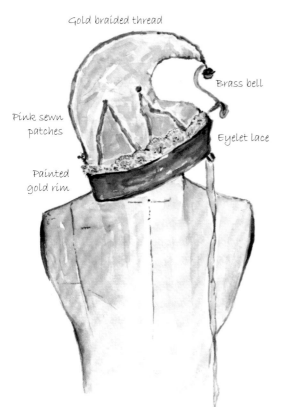

Gold braided thread

Brass bell

Pink sewn patches

Eyelet lace

Painted gold rim

MASQUERADE MASK
Dating back to the 12th century in Italy, historically for disguising the wealthy and affluent at fancy balls, so to be liberated from their own identity. In later years they evolved into a beautiful, intriguing, and mysterious accessory for social balls and festivities.

Sculptured and layered tiny white feathers

Pale pink and gray feather plumes

CHERRY ON TOP
Vintage pillbox hat, small and significant.

Crushed tulle

Cherry flowers

Dusty pink veil

Pale gold leaves

"No man, for any considerable period, can wear one face to himself and another to the multitude, without finally getting bewildered as to which may be the true."

Nathaniel Hawthorne

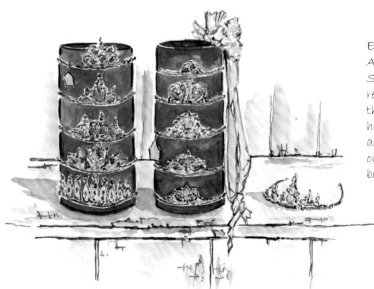

EVERY TIARA HAS A STORY
A tiara is just a little crown.
She has the perfect sparkle,
reflecting light as she illuminates
the face with her jewels. She brings
her magic to jeans and t-shirt
as well as a ballgown, enhancing
our sparkle from within to shine
brightly with an aura of charm.

ROMANTIC HEADPIECE
Glamorous, romantic, chic,
and elegant.

A WREATH OF FLOWERS
Dainty wax floral crown. Suitable
for a wedding as well as quietly
enhancing casual attire.

JEWELRY HEADPIECE
I found this when traveling in
India. Made of little mercury
beads and metal flowers woven
together with wire, all slightly
tarnished and somewhat
battered, but beautiful.

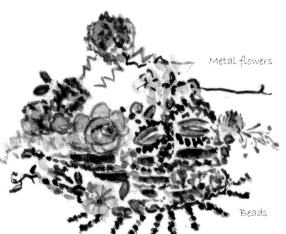

Metal flowers

Beads

PRETTY PARASOLS

Vintage parasols are another opportunity to bring prettiness, fantasy, and femininity into storytelling. In days gone by parasols were considered a fashion accessory to complement "a promenade dress or walking suit" which may explain why they are so intricate and fanciful for something considered practical.

EYE CANDY
An abundance of pink ruffles to complement the most feminine and ravishing attire.

SUNSHADES

FADED FLORAL
Timeworn while remaining subtly charming.

PASTEL SILK
Refined and genteel.

SIMPLY SHABBY
The ruffles say it all.

safely stored

Keeping our treasures safe should be as lovely as the treasures themselves. Hatboxes from the 1940s and '50s (or sometimes new) are lovely on the eyes while performing an important function.

Floral wallpaper

HATBOXES

Floral fabric

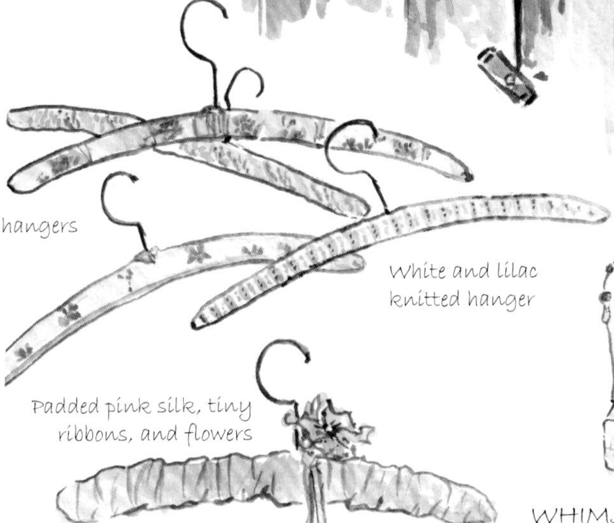

Fabric-covered hangers

White and lilac knitted hanger

Padded pink silk, tiny ribbons, and flowers

WHIMSICAL ACCOUTREMENTS
To set the stage for fantasy it helps to have whimsical accents.

My shabby-painted palette humorous elephant has graced the stage of many festivities.

MAKE BELIEVE TO HANG BY
When a prom dress isn't busy at the ball, she can be wonderfully decorative, waiting patiently hanging from a doorway or vintage armoire. To complete her beauty, she must have a hanger worthy of her.

TEARS OF THE CLOWN by Jorunn Mulen

Tomorrow is an opportunity to repaint the canvas of life's soul.
And so she transformed to blush, radiant having found herself again.

Tears of the clown 185

CLOWNS & PIERROT

I have a small collection of soulful vintage handmade clown and Pierrot costumes. There is something about their often-faded colors, floppy large ruffles, and oversized proportions that I find sweet and vulnerable. Retired from performing, with just their legacy woven into their cloth.

PINK POLKA DOT
I fell in love with this feminine pink polka dot clown costume. Somehow, she feels kind and gentle with fairy-like qualities.

Handsewn oversized double layer ruffle, with structure to hold its shape

Bias binding trim

Large floppy ruffled collar

Large fabric-covered black buttons

POIGNANT PIERROT

The sad sensitive clown. With the absence of words, his expressions are melancholy and solitary. The story of Pierrot can be traced back to a 1600s acting troop in Paris. The clown was a peasant and his love unrequited, as his fiancée favored the more jovial Harlequin.

Into the 1800s Pierrot gained stature in other art forms, both in literature and as a muse in paintings.

The simplicity of the costume evokes sensitivity, endurance, and hope.

"False face must hide what the false heart doth know."

William Shakespeare

POETIC PORTRAITS
JORUNN MULEN

When I was first introduced to Jorunn's work I immediately identified with the way she communicated an emotional expression, as though her paintings were poems, touching upon all the stages of love. She has a unique way of capturing the beautiful complexities and vulnerability of women in a way that speaks to my heart and soul. Working in her little studio in Norway, she is able to capture the magical light and intimacy evident in her work.

I consider myself a friend of Jorunn's as well as a collector of her portraits, as are many of my customers through Shabby Chic.

For this book I asked her to paint a collection with my spirit in mind, taking inspiration from the fine line of where fantasy crosses over to reality.

The monochromatic sketches in raspberry, blue, and lavender reflect a personal journey of a love of mine.

"The marks on the canvas are traces from a search. Sometimes I only know what I am looking for when I find it. In order to find it I might have to get completely lost. Some stories evolve through recognizing traces left by experience that we use to create persona. The stories may appear in layers. There is a mixture of sincerity and imagination but also a significant truth."

Jorunn Mulen

BLUE EYES
Tears, watering seeds for future love.

A FADED WISH
The illusion of permanence.

190 Dress up and make believe

PRIVATE DANCER
Dressing up and dancing on my own.

MY LOVE SONG
I thank the stars and the moon every night
for you.

BLUE BEAUTY
I loved you in-between hello and goodbye.

LAVENDER GIRL
Calm, between heartbeats.

ONLY TODAY
Yesterday is gone, tomorrow is faraway. So today, let's just kiss.

SHADOWS
My heart is confused while my eyes see the shadows. Leaving
fragrance and taste to linger until only memories remain.

KISSED LIPS
I spoke with my eyes.

BLURRY LOVE
The more she understood, the more she understood less.

LOUD SILENCE
For all we didn't say.

GYPSY WOMAN
Momentary love.

chapter 7
MY FLORAL AFFAIR

I have always had a profound appreciation for flowers.
Even as a little girl, living in a top-floor flat with a
garden, down many steps, behind the garden of the flat
below, I would visit our flowering plants as though they
were my friends. It was my imaginary playground.
I have always viewed flowers as teachers of life,
metaphorically speaking.

The simple notion that we reap what we sow leads us to
understand the unique needs of nurturing each flower.
To make space and remove unnecessary weeds that will
prevent growth. There is a time and effort for planting,
time for inspiration through budding and blooming,
and then time for rest, to dream during the times
of nothingness.

As is expressed in the Wabi Sabi philosophy, the beauty
in flowers reminds us that everything is impermanent,
imperfect, and incomplete.

"A garden to walk in and immensity to dream in—what more could
he ask? A few flowers at his feet and above him the stars."

Victor Hugo

ETERNAL BEAUTY
I admired this at a garden wedding. It spoke to me, as a never-ending beautiful love.
Delicate flowers supporting each other forever as they step into the world beyond.

GRATEFUL GARDEN

I have an abundant pastel garden at my home in California, USA. It is
not a manicured garden but there is an order to the chaos. I speak to
my flowers with compassion when they appear to be struggling. And
I speak to them with great gratitude when they bear me gifts. Some of
the flowers live their full lives in the garden, never to be cut. And others
come into my home, spreading their fragrance and gloriousness
whether in a single bud vase or as a glamorous bouquet.

ROSES

Considered by flower lovers the fairest flower of all
and a symbol of love.

When gazing at a rose, I am mesmerized at the
complexities and varieties, all under the beautiful
magical name of a "rose."

Beyond their beauty they bring intoxicating fragrances
that fill a room or subtly waft when passing by.

It's hard to say which is my most favorite,
but I do love cabbage roses, named for
their densely packed swirl of petals.
First developed by Dutch breeders
in the 17th century, their fragrance
and opulent size have made them
a favorite for us all. Mainly in
many shades of pink, as well
as soft yellow, white, and purple.
All completely romantic. I love the
inconsistency of how their branches
bow and the scale of their varied blooms.
I rarely mix roses with other flowers when
I'm "flower plopping" as I like to leave them
alone in their own wonderful world.

YVES PIAGET

I love this one for her rippled and
ruffled leaves, particularly in
raspberry shades fading to pale pink.

DIVAS LAY SLEEPING
I laid these peonies like brush strokes on a painting.

PEONIES
The classic diva. Peonies bring grace into the garden. Sometimes confused with cabbage roses for her generous globular petals. When I see a bush of Sarah Bernhardt peonies I always think of ballerinas in tutus. Late spring or early summer are the times to enjoy this breathtaking flower. A vase overflowing with lush peonies is glamorous and timeless, and commands to be the star of her own show.

MY FAVORITE PEONIES:

Sarah Bernhardt— Abundant, open, and the perfect pale pink.

Reine Hortense— Apple blossom pink, white with pink streaks.

Rubra Plena— Silky rich crimson petals.

Alba Plena— Layers on layers of ruffled white petals.

"First tend to your own garden. As your fragrant blooms open,
winds will carry your lovely seeds to the world."

Sonya Rothwell

TISSUE PETAL RANUNCULI

A rose-like blossom with layers of tissue thin petals. A rainbow of colors: pink, burgundy, orange, pale yellow, and white. Italian ranunculi are the most splendorous. In handsome midnight purple with contrasting edges of the petals in soft pink they are overflowing with romance. Ranunculi are a signature in my vases, they last forever, and their beauty remains longer still as their tissue petals dry and fade gracefully.

FLOUNCY SWEET PEAS

Delicate little flowers where I feel fairies may sleep.

Prettiest of palettes. I mostly place in groupings of jam jars for their simplicity.

A gentle little soul symbolizing gratefulness, goodbyes, and blissful pleasure.

LILACS

One of the first flowers of spring, often near Easter time. Usually just a fleeting visit of two weeks. Mostly known for being the color of their name, however there are varieties of other colors, and I love white lilacs too. I like knowing butterflies rely on lilacs for their caterpillars' survival as though they house transformation. Lilacs are perfect for my "flower plopping." I love to cut them in grand branches to make a dramatic yet still informal display.

They were the center of attention on the cover of my book **Shabby Chic Inspirations.**

HYDRANGEAS

First cultivated in Japan. An abundant flower head made up of tiny petals, with many meanings related to their color offerings. They play a welcome role in my "flower plopping," sometimes on their own but I also love to combine them with other oversized flowers, often peonies and roses.

HYDRANGEA COLOR MEANINGS:

Pink—Romance and true feelings

White—Purity and grace

Purple—Royalty

Blue—Gratitude and understanding

THE UNSUNG HERO, THE CARNATION

Carnations don't hold the same stature as roses and peonies. But to me they are a flower of great beauty and value. Often reminiscent of a sad supermarket bouquet of red and white flowers with baby's breath wrapped in plastic. But if you look a little closer at some of the spellbinding varieties, you will see carnations in a whole new light. Historically, carnations are known to have been used for the first time by Ancient Greeks and Romans for making garlands. Pink carnations are the symbol of a mother's love.

THREE TYPES OF CARNATION:

Large: One flower on stem

Spray: Lots of small flowers on a stem

Dwarf: Several small flowers with fringed edges

PREFERRED COLORS:

Loup— My all-time favorite with her light purple ground and thick creamy white picotee (picotee is a term for petals with contrasting edge).

Brava— Pure white.

Copacabana— Ballet slipper pink.

Hugo— Pale pink with white picotee.

Jacqueline Ann— White with powder coating of pink.

Apple Tea— Creamy pale yellow with little brush strokes of hot pink.

CLEMATIS

A whimsical flowering vine. She has a wonderful ability to climb up walls and around trellises. Symbolically, she represents the beauty of mental strength.

FRENCH DOUBLE TULIPS

I don't typically gravitate to
tulips, due to their uniformity
but after I once mistakenly took
a Double Late Tulip to be a peony,
I had a whole new appreciation.

They have amazing blooms and are known
as the peony-like tulip, spanning up to a
4in (10cm) spread across their multi petals,
often offering a sweet fragrance. They show
their beauty in late spring.

MY FAVORITE TULIPS:

Purple Jacket—Vibrant deep purple petals.
Charming and romantic.

Blue Diamond—Double set of petals,
impressive deep violet palette

Lilac Perfection—Densely packed lilac
purple petals

Carnaval de Nice—Oversized double set of
white petals splashed with burgundy
resembling a raspberry ripple.

DANCING DAHLIAS

Dahlias are unrivaled for their
showy displays.

They can be as tiny as 2in (5cm) in diameter
and as grand as 12in (30.5cm).

Informal decorative dahlias are the crème de la
crème to me, with their flat petals, sometimes
slightly rolled at the edges with irregular
arrangement of formation. Formal decorative
dahlias are also lovely, still with flat petals,
but arranged more regularly throughout.
Once cut, her life span is only a few days,
a brief showstopper.

MY FAVORITE DAHLIAS:

Otto's Thrill—Spectacularly eye catching.
Spanning the size of a dinner plate (10-12in
[25.5-30.5cm]) with illuminous pink blooms.
She looks stunning floating in a shallow
vintage bowl.

Café au Lait—Magnificent creamy blossoms
tinged in a light peachy pink whisper.

LEFTOVERS

As flowers transition through their cycle of life,
there are many chapters of loveliness to be had.
Starting from the garden they grew in, cut for a
bouquet, and finally their final stage as leftover
dried petals. When I was in Asia, I was inspired by the offerings
of flower petals in little bowls, left at sacred places. I have taken
to making my own offerings with leftover petals in vintage
saucers, sprinkled with water. I place them near my front door,
in a nook, or in a hallway. Gentle moments to pause and give
gratitude. And then once the leftovers are leftover, pressing petals
between tissue or watercolor paper makes them a "forever-to-keep"
token of love to pass on or to keep for yourself.

GYPSY FLOWERS

Wildflowers are nature's true gift. They plant themselves, along with their companions creating music for our eyes. They have an ephemeral beauty where they appear in their glory and then disappear, while their seeds blow in the wind and they find a new place to grow. They are a gentle reminder of the cycle of life. There is a profound pleasure from connecting to beauty that is wild and free.

Walking through a forest or an open meadow of wildflowers is a perfect meditation for the soul, absorbing the fleeting beauty, and it is most certainly where fairies play.

Wildflowers grow in uncultivated soil and different flowers bloom depending on the place in the world, creating their poetry as they sow.

SOME OF MY FAVORITE WILDFLOWERS:

Dog Rose—A scrambling beauty adorning hedges with her pale pink petals.

Cow Parsley—Gracing the roadside of the English countryside, similar to Queen Anne's lace.

Common Dog Violet—A flash of purple petals, a sanctuary for butterflies in the woodlands.

Early Purple Orchids (along with other wild orchids)— One of the first wild orchids to arrive in spring. Pretty purple.

Buttercups and Daisies— Innocent carpet of yellow and white.

Campanula—The most divine purple bush, generous with petals. The most magical installation in my book, **My Floral Affair.**

Bluebell—The enchanting violet glow is a wildflower haven, a favorite with the fairies.

Bramble—Generously bearing gifts of berries.

FLOWER PLOPPING

I do not credit myself with being a floral designer. I have met many who I admire for their artistry and I love observing their techniques in creating their vision, from the flowers they choose, to their tools, including secateurs (flower cutters), clear tape, and wire. Their designs are natural art pieces. However, I am a simple "flower plopper." This is my special technique of gathering my stems, plopping them in a vase, and letting them fall as they may. I'm never disappointed in how they find their voice, naturally and with ease. I am less intimidated if I just have a selection of beautiful vases, my favorite flowers, and my instincts. And that is my recipe for certain success.

I have a wonderful collection of vintage vases acquired from flea markets and second-hand stores. Frilly and romantic, stylishly simple, teeny and grand. I consider a vase a temple in which to house flowers. Part of my collection includes dinnerware pieces such as sugar bowls with lost lids and chipped creamers, all finding a new sense of purpose. Being called into service, like they are coming back from being retired.

Sometimes the vases I choose to accompany my flowers are an extension to the story of the blossoms, so they blend. Sometimes I like a twist of color. If all the elements are beautiful, the destiny of something wonderful is always guaranteed.

BLUE, WHITE & PINK
Floppy pink roses supported in folksy pitcher with raised blue floral embellishments.

The pitcher itself is cracked; a glass liner holds water.

BRISTOL VASE

Wide ruffled opening

Hand-painted flowers

Due to manufacturing technique there are inherent imperfections

BUTTERFLIES
Hand-painted butterfly vase, with narrow opening, welcoming only a few stems so as not to distract from the details.

WHITE RUFFLES
This opaque white glass vase with ruffled opening neutrally receives any array of blooms.

CAKE BOUQUET
Roughly applied
butter frosting is the
stage for scattered
blossoms and blooms.

OVERSIZED TEMPLES
Faded florals blend with faded
flowers. A nice grouping.

TINY GOLD EGG CUP
I would always include an egg
cup with a flower on a tray
accompanying breakfast in bed.

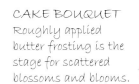

SUBTLE
Delicate floral details, whimsy
and traditional.

CHIPPED BUT REGAL
Gold accented creamer,
damaged but still royal.

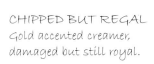

MY SOUL SISTER
LAURENCE AMÉLIE

Laurence Amélie is an artist living and painting in her idyllic Waterlily Cottage near Fontainebleau in France. Over the years Laurence has traveled numerous times to Los Angeles to stay with me, where for two months she paints her beloved abstract floral and tutu paintings for her passionate American collectors. I have a large barn at my Californian home, nestled in my rose garden, which I convert into a painting studio for her visits. When Laurence paints, her heart and the paint on her brush are one and her process of painting is a beautiful mess, so in preparation I cover my floors and everything else in sight with tarps to give her freedom without concern of splashes. As the days pass during her visits, her shoes and clothes blend into her palette, and get covered in splashes of paints. Sometimes carrying through into my home, to this day I treasure a blob of hot pink paint that somehow found its way onto a crystal drop on my chandelier.

Laurence spends days preparing the background of her canvases, applying layers of acrylic paint in multiple tones which build depth to each piece. She is inspired by the California light and her walks through my rambling rose garden to the barn. The magic and ethereal quality of each of Laurence's paintings are in the movement she creates portraying the illusion of the flowers in a gentle breeze.

The romance of Laurence's work is the essence of Shabby Chic, speaking the same language in a pastel palette as well as passionate darker tones.

For this book I asked Laurence for a collection of flowers on watercolor paper which she painted with watered-down acrylic paint. Laurence says when painting in this medium, "my spirit feels like a butterfly, I feel a magical and invisible link and just let the brushes and watery paint go." I see this collection as having a transparent quality of poetry with flowers.

"I paint what moves me, flowers growing haphazardly in poetic disorder. Leaving free access to my imagination, where my subconscious will delight, splash to splash, accidents from my unfettered brush. Each canvas ending up almost acquiring a soul."

Laurence Amélie

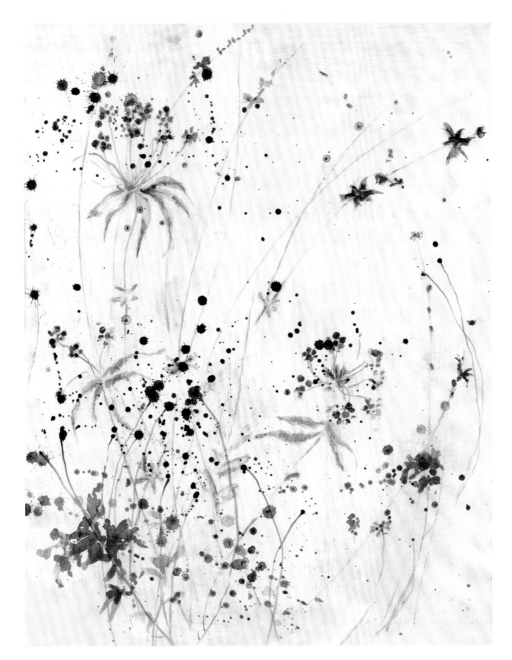

STARDUST FLOWERS

"Every artist dips his brush in his own soul, and
paints his own nature into his pictures."

Henry Ward Beecher

My soul sister—Laurence Amélie 211

DAISIES
"Eyes of the day."
Opening in the light of day and
folding in her petals as night falls.

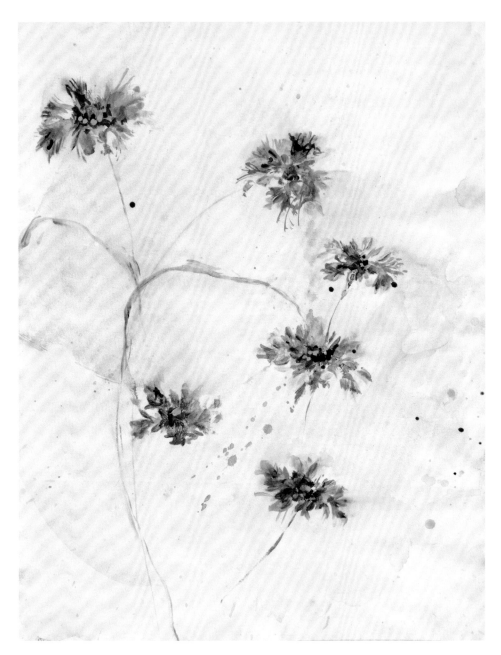

CORNFLOWER BLUE

From a weed to a flower.

Once upon a time a weed amongst cornfields.

Now considered a cherished flower in her own right.

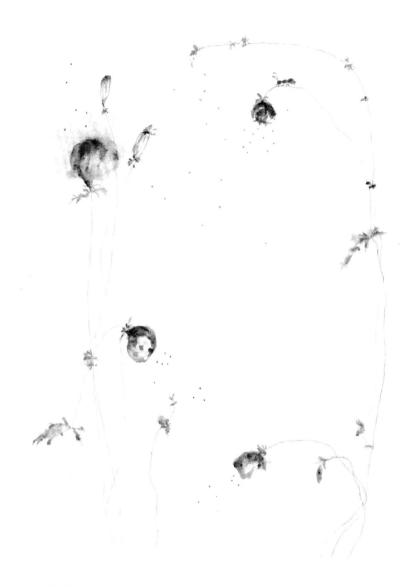

ROSE BUDS

"The roses under my window make no reference to former roses or better ones; they are what they are; they exist with God today. There is no time to them. There is simply the rose; it is perfect in every moment of its existence."

Ralph Waldo Emerson

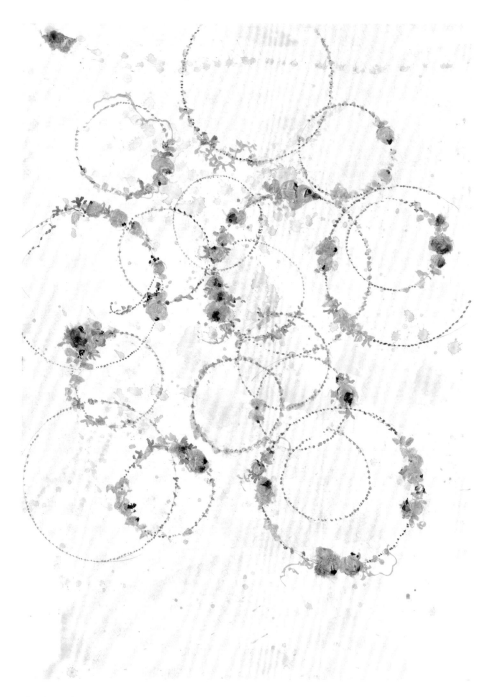

ETERNAL ROSES
The beauty lies in the space in-between.

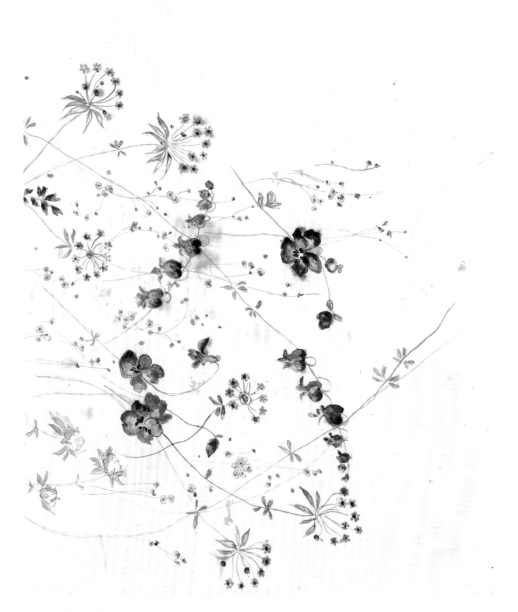

FORGET-ME-NOT
"Silently, one by one, in the infinite meadows of heaven,
Blossomed the lovely stars, the forget-me-nots of the angels."
Henry Wadsworth Longfellow

WILDFLOWERS

"To see a World in a Grain of Sand
And a Heaven in a Wild Flower,
Hold Infinity in the palm of your hand
And Eternity in an hour."

William Blake

index

Sonya Rothwell (pages 222-223) is an artist and a friend of mine and romantic free spirit. She lives in England in a National Trust manor built circa 1730, surrounded by an enchanted garden, which Sonya describes as her solace and inspiration. It's where she begins her days, strolling and noticing every detail of Mother Nature. The quietude and stillness of the garden bring her peace and inspire her ideas. For this book I wanted to include a piece from her series "As the Birds" painted on watercolor with liquid pencil. Her birds in flight against a sky of shades of pink evoke a sense of freedom and faith as we travel on life's beautiful journey.

resources

ARTISTS

RACHEL ASHWELL SHABBY CHIC
shabbychic.com
@rachelashwell

SHABBY CHIC STORE
1013 Montana Avenue,
Santa Monica, CA 90403, USA

BEN PECK-WHISTON
(all sketches)
benpeckwhiston.com
@benpeckwhiston

JORUNN MULEN
(pages 184–185, 188–197)
jorunn-mulen.com
@jorunnmulen

LAURENCE AMÉLIE
(pages 96–97, 119, and 210–219)
laurence-amelie.com
@laurence.amelie

KIM MCCARTY
(pages 126–135)
kimmccarty.net
@kimchimccarty

SONYA ROTHWELL
(pages 222–223)
gallerybeautiful.com
@gallery.beautiful

DESIGNER'S TREASURES FEATURED

PEARL LOWE
(pages 29 and 40)
pearllowe.co.uk
@pearllowe

SERA LOFTUS
(page 46)
seraoflondon.com
@seraoflondon

LAURA TAYLOR
(title page)
etsy.com/shop/thisritualvintage
@this.ritual

GERALDINE JAMES
(page 48)
@geraldinejames01

AMANDA DAUGHTRY
(pages 19 and 84)
@mysimplehome

TANIA BOUREAU
(page 179)
etsy.com/shop/grangedecharmeart
@grange_de_charme

FORTNUM & MASON
(page 93)
181 Piccadilly, St. James's,
London W1A 1ER, UK
fortnumandmason.com
@fortnums

KENSINGTON PALACE
(page 92)
Kensington Gardens,
London W8 4PX, UK
hrp.org.uk/kensington-palace

DIPTYQUE
(page 89)
diptyqueparis.com
@diptyque

SANTA MARIA NOVELLA
(page 89)
buy.smnovella.com
@santamarianovella1612

JP WEAVER
(ornamental molding, pages 109
and 114)
jpweaver.com

AMERICAN TIN CEILINGS
(page 111)
americantinceilings.com
@americantinceilings

FAVORITE PLACES TO TREASURE HUNT

LARK VINTAGE, HAYLEY NOAD
(page 31)
larkvintage.co.uk
@larkvintage

KEMPTON PARK ANTIQUE MARKET
sunburyantiques.com/kempton
Kempton Park Racecourse,
Staines Road East, Sunbury on
Thames TW16 5AQ, UK

SHEPTON MALLET FLEA MARKET
sheptonflea.com
Royal Bath & West Showground,
Shepton Mallet,
Somerset BA4 6QN, UK

PORTOBELLO ROAD ANTIQUES MARKET
portobelloroadantiques.com
Portobello Road, London W11, UK

THE FROME INDEPENDENT
5/6 Palmer Street, Frome,
Somerset BA11 1DS, UK
thefromeindependent.org.uk
@thefromeindependent

DAIRY HOUSE ANTIQUES
Station Road, Semley, Shaftesbury,
Dorset SP7 9AN, UK
dairyhouseantiques.com
@dairyhouseantiques

ROUND TOP ANTIQUE MARKET
roundtoptexasantiques.com
@roundtopantiquestexas

BRIMFIELD
thebrimfieldshow.com
@thebrimfieldshow

eBay

Etsy

Endpaper art by Laurence Amélie

"Like a small, seemingly fragile migratory bird, battling the elements day into night, I fly onwards and upwards, thanking life for empowering me in this curious way."

Sonya Rothwell

acknowledgments

This book is a silver lining of the pandemic lockdown. During those long quiet months I was drawn to recording my thoughts and philosophies and opted for sketches and art in lieu of photography which would not have been possible during that time. As my meandering thoughts unfolded, Ben Peck-Whiston worked diligently on magical sketches, while Jorunn Mulen and Laurence Amélie produced thought-provoking collections of art. And Kim McCarty and Sonya Rothwell lent me works from their archives to complete my vision of My Painted Stories. I thank all these talented, generous, and soulful artists for their heartfelt contributions that have given this book inspiration and gentle love.

And I thank everyone and everything that has crossed my path on my life's journey that have in some way inspired and moved me and given me deep and meaningful thoughts to reflect upon.

And as always, thanks to all at CICO Books who continue to trust and support my vision, giving me the freedom to express myself.